D0198416

Russia, America and the Cold War, 1949–1991

MARTIN McCAULEY

Longman

An imprint of Pearson Education

Harlow, England · London · New York · Reading, Massachusetts · San Francisco
Toronto · Don Mills, Ontario · Sydney · Tokyo · Singapore · Hong Kong · Seoul
Taipei · Cape Town · Madrid · Mexico City · Amsterdam · Munich · Paris · Milan

Pearson Education Limited
Edinburgh Gate
Harlow, Essex CM20 2JE
England

and Associated Companies throughout the world

Visit us on the World Wide Web at:
www.pearson.com

© Addison Wesley Longman Limited 1998

The right of Martin McCauley to be identified
as the author of this Work has been asserted by him
in accordance with the Copyright, Designs and
Patents Act 1988.

All Rights reserved; no part of this publication may be
reproduced, stored in a retrieval system, or transmitted
in any form or by any means, electronic, mechanical,
photocopying, recording, or otherwise without the
prior written permission of the Publishers or a licence
permitting restricted copying in the United Kingdom
issued by the Copyright Licensing Agency Ltd.,
90 Tottenham Court Road, London W1T 4LP.

First published 1998

ISBN 0 582 27936 4 Paper

British Library Cataloguing-in-Publication Data

A catalogue record for this book is
available from the British Library

Library of Congress Cataloging-in-Publication Data
McCauley, Martin.
    Russia, America, and the cold war, 1949–1991 / Martin McCauley.
        p.   cm. -- (Seminar studies in history)
    Includes bibliographical references (P. NNN) and index.
    ISBN 0-582-27936-4
    1. United States--Foreign relations--Soviet Union. 2. Soviet
Union--Foreign relations--United States. 3. United States--Foreign
relations--1945–1989. 4. Cold War. I. Series
    E183.8.S65M3745 1998
    327.73047--dc21
                                                                    98-3445
                                                                    CIP

10   9
05   04

Set by 7 in 10/12 Sabon Roman
Printed in Malaysia, PP

CONTENTS

AN INTRODUCTION TO THE SERIES

Such is the pace of historical enquiry in the modern world that there is an ever-widening gap between the specialist article or monograph, incorporating the results of current research, and general surveys, which inevitably become out of date. *Seminar Studies in History* are designed to bridge this gap. The series was founded by Patrick Richardson in 1966 and his aim was to cover major themes in British, European and World history. Between 1980 and 1996 Roger Lockyer continued his work, before handing the editorship over to Clive Emsley and Gordon Martel. Clive Emsley is Professor of History at the Open University, while Gordon Martel is Professor of History at the University of Northern British Columbia, Canada and Senior Research Fellow at De Montfort University.

All the books are written by experts in their field who are not only familiar with the latest research but have often contributed to it. They are frequently revised, in order to take account of new information and interpretations. They provide a selection of documents to illustrate major themes and provoke discussion, and also a guide to further reading. The aim of *Seminar Studies* is to clarify complex issues without over-simplifying them, and to stimulate readers into deepening their knowledge and understanding of major themes and topics.

ACKNOWLEDGEMENTS

The publishers would like to thank the following for permission to reproduce copyright material: Akademie Verlag GmbH for extracts from *Jahrbuch fur Historische Kommunismusforschung* by Dashichev; Faber and Faber for extracts from *Kennedy v. Khrushchev, The Crisis Years 1960–63* by Michael R. Beschloss; Weidenfeld and Nicolson for extracts from *The White House Years* by Henry Kissinger.

Whilst every effort has been made to trace owners of copyright material, in a few cases this has proved to be problematic and we take this opportunity to offer our apologies to any copyright holders whose rights we may have unwittingly infringed.

NOTE ON REFERENCING SYSTEM

Readers should note that numbers in square brackets [5] refer them to the corresponding entry in the Bibliography at the end of the book (specific page references are given in italic). A number in square brackets preceded by *Doc.* [*Doc.* 5] refers readers to the corresponding item in the Document section which follows the main text.

NOTE ON THE TEXT

Throughout this book, America and the United States, and Russia and the Soviet Union, are used interchangeably. The country now known as Russia or the Russian Federation is referred to as the Russian Federation in this text.

LIST OF MAPS

PART ONE: THE BACKGROUND

1 THE COLD WAR IN PERSPECTIVE

The term 'Cold War' was popularised by the US columnist Walter Lippmann and entered general usage in 1947. The Truman doctrine, proclaimed in March 1947, underlined US willingness to help counter the communist threat in Greece and Turkey, but in reality, it was a general commitment to come to the aid of states facing a communist takeover. Its economic arm, the Marshall Plan, announced in June 1947, was to provide aid and thereby to revive the flagging market economies of Europe. Economic prosperity was perceived as the most effective antidote to the attractiveness of communism.

The expression 'cold war' had been coined by the fourteenth-century Spanish writer Don Juan Manuel. He was describing the conflict between Christendom and Islam and observed that hot and cold wars were mainly distinguishable by the ways they ended. 'War that is very fierce and very hot ends either with death or peace, whereas a cold war neither brings peace nor confers honour on those who wage it.' Before 1990 neither east nor west had proved victorious, but communists could point to the reunification of Vietnam in 1975 as evidence that the tide was flowing in their direction. The other partitions which symbolised the conflict – Germany and Korea – remained. But in 1990 the tide seemed to be turning, as the communist regime in East Germany fell and Germany was reunited. Then in 1991 came the unexpected collapse of the Soviet Union. One of the reasons for this collapse was that the economic burden of being a superpower became unbearable. The Soviet Union imploded. The irony was that the last President of the Soviet Union, Mikhail Gorbachev, had brought the Cold War to an end, realising that his country could not sustain it any longer. In doing so he destroyed his own state. By the late 1990s only the division of Korea remains as testament to past tensions.

The Cold War can be divided into four main periods. The first, Cold War I, spans the last years of Stalin and concludes with his death in 1953. Russian foreign policy during these years was low-risk or risk-averse. Then follows the second period, one of danger and confrontation, from the death of Stalin until détente breaks out in 1969. Central to this is the high-risk diplomacy of Khrushchev who was much too confident of the Soviet Union's growing power. Then follows the third period, one of détente and the desire of both superpowers to normalise their relations and reduce the risk of confrontation. This era ends with the misjudged Soviet invasion of Afghanistan in 1979, arguably the most disastrous mistake Moscow made in foreign policy during the whole Soviet era. Russian advisers even informed their leaders that the continued Soviet presence in Afghanistan could lead to a Third World War [*Doc. 11*]. The ensuing fourth period, Cold War II, saw an acceleration in the arms race and a rising political temperature. This was only halted by the fresh vision of Gorbachev, who wanted to reassess fundamentally the goals of foreign policy and to negotiate a new relationship with America, one which would remove ideology from Russian foreign policy formation. Moscow would no longer support communism and national liberation movements around the globe, and interdependence became a guiding light of Moscow's policy as it set out to build a new world order in partnership with Washington. However, all the gains accrued to America, and the demise of the Soviet Union followed swiftly on the end of the Cold War.

COLD WAR I

Some scholars regard the Cold War as beginning in 1917 when the Bolsheviks established the first communist state. As early as 1918 Lenin had sought an accommodation (co-habitation) with the capitalist world, believing that the preservation of Soviet power was a key element in promoting world revolution. Soviet foreign policy until the outbreak of the Second World War was therefore defensive. However, Stalin subscribed to the Marxist belief that war between capitalism and communism was inevitable eventually, so the Soviet Union had to become militarily strong enough to win such a conflict. Given this and the expectation that wars would be fought on foreign territory, Soviet military doctrine was offensive.

The Second World War transformed Russia into the leading European military power and a great power, an actor on the world stage for the first time. Its only real rival was America and managing the relationship with Washington assumed vital significance for Moscow. In 1945 a partnership for peace appeared possible. Moscow played a full role in the negotiations which led to the formation of the

International Monetary Fund (IMF) and the World Bank, and positive analyses of the benefits of membership were being forwarded to Stalin as late as December 1945. However, the IMF stipulation that its employees should have access to sensitive economic data, including gold reserves, before any loan could be extended proved too much for Moscow. Stalin did not want the west to realise how weak economically the Soviet Union was in 1945.

In the aftermath of the war, Stalin did not wish to provoke a conflict with America and ordered communist parties in Europe to participate in government wherever possible, for example in France and Italy, but not to attempt to seize power. The strongly anti-communist British Foreign Secretary, Ernest Bevin, was alarmed at the waxing of communist influence. As early as 1946 he was prepared to accept the division of Europe, but it had to appear that the Russians were to blame. The consolidation of communist power in eastern and south-eastern Europe in 1946, and the possibility that the communists would win the civil war in Greece, eventually led to the Truman doctrine and the Marshall Plan.

Moscow saw the world divided into two antagonistic camps, the socialist and the capitalist, with countries such as India and Indonesia outside both. The communist take-over in Czechoslovakia in February 1948, more due to miscalculations by local politicians than to Moscow's machinations, convinced many in the west that the communist steamroller was moving westwards. The Berlin blockade, which began in June 1948, a bad miscalculation by Stalin, added fuel to the flames. A direct result of the blockade was the establishment of West Germany and, almost immediately afterwards, of the German Democratic Republic in the east. The founding of the People's Republic of China in October 1949 brought into being a second potential communist giant. In response to this situation NATO was formed at the request of the west Europeans. In June 1950, there were further communist advances in Asia, as North Korea invaded South Korea, and in Vietnam the communists went on the offensive, against the French and defeated them finally at Dien Bien Phu in 1954.

BRINKMANSHIP

The death of Stalin in March 1953 and the election of President Eisenhower, committed to ending the Korean War, signalled a phase of negotiation between east and west and the ending of Cold War I. Moscow had already launched the doctrine of peaceful co-existence in 1952, following the successful explosion of its atomic bomb. War ceased to be inevitable because it was so destructive. The Russians toyed with the concept of a united, neutral Germany, but this was opposed by West Germany and France. An armistice was signed in Korea in July 1953, and a cease-fire in Indo-China in 1954. A new mood of optimism was abroad and negotiations between east and west were held in 1954 and 1955, the first since 1947, covering Germany, Austria, Korea and Indo-China. The Soviets agreed to leave Austria, with the peace treaty describing Austria as a neutral state. There was no agreement on Germany but Moscow held to its goal of a united, neutral Germany until 1958, when Khrushchev declared that the socialist achievements of the GDR could not be negotiated away. Korea and Vietnam also remained divided, as there was no victor in the contest between capitalism and communism.

This optimism soon lapsed, however, and the period 1953–69 became one of dangerous conflicts and brinkmanship, with relations between east and west quite volatile. The Hungarian uprising and the Anglo-French invasion of Egypt occurred in 1956, and the latter led to the Russians threatening to intervene on the Egyptian side. Another period of negotiations was initiated by Khrushchev's visit to America in 1959, and the emergence of the Camp David spirit (an early version of détente) between him and Eisenhower, but this ended abruptly in 1960 at the Paris summit, which was wrecked by the fall-out from the Russian shooting down of an American U2 reconnaissance aircraft. Relations continued frosty in 1961 in the wake of the Laos and Berlin crises (which saw the erection of the Berlin Wall).

The most dangerous incident turned out to be the Cuban missile crisis of October 1962, which brought the world close to nuclear war. It resulted from the over-optimism of Khrushchev, who believed that the final victory of communism over capitalism was in sight and that he had the measure of President John F. Kennedy. Whereas Stalin had been a low-risk negotiator, Khrushchev was a high-risk negotiator, although he did eventually back down in the face of a critical situation. The crisis had a sobering effect, with a nuclear test ban treaty signed in 1963 and a hotline between Moscow and Washington established. When Khrushchev was removed in 1964, Kosygin took over as chief negotiator and summits continued until 1967.

Tensions were high elsewhere in the world. In 1965 the US took the fateful decision to intervene in Vietnam, and also went into the Dominican Republic. The third Arab-Israeli war erupted in 1967, with the Soviet Union and the US committed to opposing sides. The 1968 Warsaw Pact invasion of Czechoslovakia – after President

Johnson had assured Moscow that the country was within the latter's sphere of influence – spread fear in West Germany and raised tension elsewhere. It also split western communist parties and fatally weakened the attractiveness of Soviet socialism. This era of brinkmanship eventually came to a close with the advent of President Nixon in 1969, beginning a sustained period of negotiations, called détente.

DÉTENTE

This phase lasted a decade, from 1969 to 1979, and produced many accords. The recognition by the US that the Soviet Union and the US enjoyed nuclear parity led to the SALT-I agreement in 1972. The Conference on Security and Co-operation in Europe (CSCE) in 1975 finished with the signing of the Helsinki Final Act. The Soviets attained one goal – the recognition of the inviolability of the post-1945 frontiers in Europe – but acknowledged that human rights were a matter for legitimate international concern. The Paris Accords permitted the US to withdraw its troops from Indo-China and close an unhappy chapter in its history. Détente ended in 1979 with the Soviet invasion of Afghanistan, although it had already been the butt of conservative critics in the US for conceding too much to Moscow. The move into Afghanistan was the result of two Soviet miscalculations: that the operation would only take a few weeks and that the Americans would not raise any major objections. President Carter confessed that the invasion had opened his eyes about the real nature of the Soviet Union.

COLD WAR II AND THE END OF THE COLD WAR

Cold War II covered the period from the invasion of Afghanistan to the advent of Mikhail Gorbachev in March 1985. It was marked by rapidly rising military expenditures as both sides spoke of the need to be prepared for war should the other side strike. War became more likely. Hence the use of force in international relations became legitimate. In the US President Reagan promised to restore military superiority, making it clear that he was willing to intervene in Third World states, such as Libya, Cuba and Nicaragua, to promote pro-western values. The Soviets responded in kind and, among other things, installed SS20s in eastern Europe. The influence of the Soviet military on security policy in the late Brezhnev period was unprecedented.

The temperature of the polemics between east and west during this period was reminiscent of Cold War I. The Soviet Union was pilloried and described as the 'evil empire' by President Reagan, and was also accused of supporting international terrorism and even attempting to assassinate the Pope. Washington began to see Moscow's hand behind all the unrest throughout the world. Superpower relations became a zero sum game: if the Soviet Union gained an advantage anywhere then the US was the loser, and vice versa. One of the reasons for this was the wave of communist states which had come into existence in and after 1974 in the Middle East, Africa and Central America. The United States and its allies determined to redress the balance. The US used trade boycotts (for example, ending grain shipments to the USSR) as a weapon and pulled out of the 1980 Olympics in Moscow. (The Soviets failed to turn up in Los Angeles in 1984.)

The arrival of Andropov as Soviet leader in 1982 elicited little change in Soviet attitudes. His belief that the peace movement was influential enough to force the West German government to rethink its policy of installing Pershing and Cruise missiles was misplaced. East–west talks continued, however, (unlike Cold War I) in Geneva on intermediate-range nuclear weapons and strategic arms reductions, in Madrid on CSCE, and in Vienna on Mutual and Balance Force Reductions in Europe.

The election of Mikhail Gorbachev as Soviet leader in March 1985 introduced a sea change to international relations. Convinced that the arms race was crippling his country, he afforded primacy to foreign policy and spoke of the new political thinking. This acknowledged that security could not be achieved by military means alone, that all states were interdependent, that nuclear weapons should be abolished by the year 2000 and that ideology should be banished from foreign and security policy-making. Together with Eduard Shevardnadze, his Foreign Minister, he launched a charm offensive and bowled the west over. His first meeting with President Reagan, in Geneva in November 1985, led to a joint statement that proposed that the superpowers' nuclear arsenal be cut by 50 per cent. The next summit took place in Reykjavik in October 1986, but on this occasion disagreement over the Strategic Defence Initiative (SDI or Star Wars) could not be overcome. The third summit, in Washington DC in December 1987, was historic. It produced an agreement to eliminate a whole category of nuclear weapons: land-based intermediate and shorter range missiles. This was the Intermediate Range Nuclear Forces (INF) Treaty, signed by Reagan and Gorbachev at their final summit in Moscow in May–June 1988. Serious difficulties continued to exist, however, especially over verification of the implementation of the treaty. The two presidents did not discuss SDI: the Soviets had conceded defeat.

One of the agreements reached at Geneva had been on the withdrawal of Soviet troops from Afghanistan, completed in February 1989. Soviet relations with President Bush were good and produced two historic agreements: the CFE treaty signed in November 1990, and the START treaty signed in July 1991. However, opposition from the Soviet General Staff undermined the CFE treaty and the dissolution of the USSR halted progress on the START treaty. The Cold War was over because the USSR had become a supplicant, with Gorbachev seeking in vain to raise vast credits in the west to shore up the old system.

Did the Cold War end in 1990 or 1991? Those who regard the Cold War as merely another term for superpower competition between Russia and America would say 1990, when Gorbachev declared it to be over. However, those who see it as a systemic struggle, between capitalism and communism, between democracy and authoritarianism, would plump for 1991, when the Soviet Union ceased to exist.

THE CHARACTERISTICS OF THE COLD WAR

During Cold War I there was a military build-up, the division of Europe and eventually the world into two camps, and no meaningful negotiations between east and west (the Soviet Union even boycotted the United Nations for a time). The conflict was restricted to Europe in the first phase and then moved to east Asia in the latter stage. Stalin wanted an accommodation with the west but was too pessimistic about the Soviet Union's ability to resist the allures of western capitalism. In eastern Europe he would probably have settled for the Finnish solution – benevolent neutrality. He always kept his options open on Germany and again would have preferred a united, neutral, benevolent Germany. The west misjudged the Soviet Union's strength and intentions, with the US initially perceiving Moscow as posing no threat to its security, then regarding it as a horrendous threat. This hysteria produced McCarthyism and deeply coloured the debate until the demise of the Soviet Union. Western Europe was weak after 1945 and fearful of the attractiveness of Marxist solutions and Soviet intentions. The Berlin blockade (Stalin could have had an advantageous agreement but overplayed his hand) reinforced western concern about Soviet expansionism. Hence, although Stalin always sought dialogue and put forward various proposals on Germany, he always met with a lukewarm response.

In the early postwar period the US was the dominant economic power and enjoyed a nuclear monopoly for a short time, but by the mid-1950s the USSR believed that it was catching up and was capable of putting America in the shade. The utopianism of Khrushchev surfaced in 1961, when he proclaimed that the foundations of a communist society (very high living standards for all) would be built by 1980. Partly because of this optimism, Soviet policy under Khrushchev became much more unpredictable and he was keen to make use of the Soviet nuclear arsenal as a bargaining chip. He sought a solution to the Berlin situation (West Berlin would gradually fall under communist control) and then acceded to the GDR wish to build the Berlin Wall. He also expanded the range of Soviet foreign policy by visiting Asia, especially India, and the Middle East and offering an alternative to western capitalism. However, it was under Khrushchev, for the first time, that the communist monolith began to crack (the Sino-Soviet conflict) and it was no longer accurate to see the world in bipolar terms. The Cuban revolution of 1959 was not communist in origin but Castro was forced to seek aid and protection from Moscow because of American threats. Later, in 1962, the Cuban missile crisis resulted from Khrushchev wishing to counter American dominance in intercontinental ballistic missiles by placing Soviet missiles on Cuba. Soviet commanders later claimed that they had authority to launch a nuclear strike on the US if they perceived they were under nuclear attack. One consequence of the Soviet climb-down was to exacerbate relations with Beijing.

Détente marked the apogee of Soviet power. It is ironic that at the moment the US conceded nuclear parity Russia began to decline economically. The late 1970s saw the influence of the Soviet military on the rise as Moscow began to get involved in the communist Third World. Post-colonial Africa appeared to welcome communism (Angola, Mozambique, for instance) and Ethiopia also joined the band. Those in the west who had been warning of Soviet expansionism seized upon the invasion of Afghanistan in 1979 to demand greater defence preparedness.

Cold War II differed from Cold War I in that by 1979 the west had lost its fear of communism as an ideology. Instead it had become a military and security threat. The violent suppression of the Prague spring had been the death knell of Marxism, and the ensuing period saw virulent propaganda campaigns, even more so than after 1946. One of the most vigorous debates was about the health of the Russian economy. It is now clear that the Russian economy was in a state of terminal decline, but at the time those who supported the vast rise in US defence spending could not concede that the Soviet Unior might collapse. There were those who believed that the most appropriate way to overcome Russia was to increase defence spending to the point where the Russians would be ruined by being forced to keep up, since the Russian GDP was about 40 per cent of the American. One of the unexpected side-effects of this eventually successful policy was a huge US budget deficit.

There are many theories about the reasons for the Cold War [27 *pp. 24–8*]:

- *The Russian threat.* All the conflicts and crises originated with the Soviet Union and were caused by Russian expansionism. This in turn was part and parcel of Marxist-Leninist ideology which envisaged the world victory of socialism over capitalism. Hence one state is blamed for all the problems which arise in international relations.

- *American imperialism.* This is the mirror image of the previous view, with Washington the root of all evil, emanating from predatory, expansionist capitalism. Again responsibility is ascribed to the actions of one state with the other trying to avoid armed conflict. Capitalism is viewed as requiring confrontation and military production to survive.

- *The superpowers theory.* Developed by the Chinese in the 1960s to demonstrate that Moscow had departed from the true Marxist-Leninist path, this view regards the superpowers as colluding and competing in an attempt to rule the world. This underlines the break between Beijing and Moscow and reveals Chinese insecurity. In the 1970s there is rapprochement with America, which in turn alarms Russia.

- *The theory of the arms race.* The build-up of nuclear weapons had reached proportions where it appeared to be out of control. Both east and west were responsible. Hence the stopping and reversing of the arms race was of paramount importance. This theory was especially popular among those in the peace movement.

- *North–south theory.* Proponents of this view perceive the main conflict in the world as that between north and south, between rich and poor nations, and between dominant and dominated states. The contest for the leading position in the Third World is the motive behind all conflict.

- *West–west theory.* World politics is dominated by conflicts among rich capitalist states. The Russian-American conflict is a smoke screen for the real conflict: that between the US, Japan and the European Union. The origins of Cold War II are to be found in the increasingly sharp conflicts among rich capitalist states. These, in turn, promote and exacerbate conflicts within the Third World.

- *Intra-state theory.* The domestic policies of states determine their foreign policy. Changes in foreign policy are related to movements in internal power relations, new economic weaknesses and alterations in social composition. Politicians use international events to resolve internal tensions and overcome domestic competitors.

- *Class conflict.* This is based on the Marxist analysis of class conflict as the motor of change. Tension is the product of the ebb and flow of social revolution. The conflict between capitalism and communism is expressed in tensions between the superpowers. The revolutionary movement in the Third World inevitably sucks in the superpowers.

The various explanations listed above can be accompanied by other ways of analysing the reasons for the Cold War [49 *pp. 9–30*]:

- *The orthodox or traditional view.* This corresponds to the Russian threat thesis above. Russia was always hostile to the west and only co-operated when it was tactically necessary. It was, by definition, an expansionary power.

- *The revisionist view.* This adopts the same analysis as the thesis about American imperialism above.

- *Post-revisionist interpretations.* These seek to avoid monocausal reasons for conflict and overcome the weaknesses of the above two views. The orthodox interpretation pays little attention to the legitimate security needs of Russia and the revisionist fails to lay stress on changes in Russian approaches which led to changes in American policy. Access to official documents led to a flood of post-revisionist studies which attempt to achieve some detachment from the conflict and assess the responsibility of both sides for the tension. These studies can be called post-revisionist (mark 1).

The post-revisionist (mark 2) approach is by John Lewis Geddis who, while taking into consideration the above studies, develops a sophisticated analysis based on containment before and after Kennan (see below) [16]. America and Britain needed Russia as an ally to defeat Germany, but in so doing created another threat to their security. Containment, the term used to describe American policy towards Russia after 1945, may be viewed as an attempt to cope with the consequences of the bargain entered into during the Second World War. The goal of containment was to ensure that Russia did not reshape the international order in such a manner as to make it hostile to the west. The term 'containment' was coined by George Kennan in July 1947, when he advocated a 'long-term, patient but firm and vigilant containment of Russian expansive tendencies'. This led to the Truman doctrine and the Marshall Plan. The US administration had no desire to oppose communism on a world scale, only expansionary Soviet communism, and began to use the term 'totalitarian' rather than 'communist'.

Halliday's view [27] can be classified as a post-revisionist (mark 3) analysis. He reveals the weaknesses of the Russian threat and American imperialist interpretations. Whereas analyses of the Cold War during the 1940s have concentrated on Russian-American rivalry for influence, the conflict gradually spread until it embraced the whole world. Hence this study of the Cold War, beginning in 1949, will consider superpower rivalry throughout the world. The bipolar world of the 1940s became a multipolar world from the 1950s onwards [17; 47; 48; 52; 57; 67; 69; 70].

PART TWO: DESCRIPTIVE ANALYSIS

2 COLD WAR I: 1949–1953

THE BERLIN BLOCKADE

The first time that war between Russia and America became a possibility was during the Berlin blockade. Stalin's response to the fusing of the western zones of Germany, the end of de-Nazification, the resurrection of German industrial power and the introduction of the German mark (Deutsche Mark or DM) in June 1948 was defensive. His advisers had not envisaged that West Berlin could be supplied by air so he felt confident that the western allies would eventually be forced to leave West Berlin. Stalin's goal was to ensure communist control over all Berlin and end access by the western powers, as had been agreed by Russia, America, Britain and France in 1945. The Russians began interfering with traffic to West Berlin but on 24 June imposed a ban on all traffic flows. In response, the American military in West Germany advocated the use of military force to clear the routes to Berlin. There were those in the US air force who did not believe that West Berlin could be supplied by air.

President Truman decided not to risk war in an election year, but he had to appear tough and not be seen to be caving in to Stalin, particularly since the fall of Czechoslovakia in February 1948 fuelled the arguments of the American right that communism was on the march. The resultant Berlin airlift was a spectacular success, with the allied air forces keeping the western part of the city alive. At its peak, they flew in 13,000 tons of supplies daily, and kept going for 324 days. Stalin's emissaries in Berlin reported that they expected the airlift to fail and this may have misled Stalin into continuing the blockade. He eventually conceded defeat in May 1949, but the conflict changed Russian-American relations. There was a general feeling in America that if war had come, the atomic bomb would have been used. Neither Moscow nor Washington wanted war but both now prepared for war. The two leading world powers had clearly become adversaries and the term 'cold war' is an apt description of their relations from this point.

The airlift transformed Harry Truman's political fortunes. Trailing badly in the race for the presidency with the Republican Thomas E. Dewey, he gradually caught up and surprised most analysts by winning. The conflict over Berlin allowed him to demonstrate that he was a strong, resolute leader, a man who could stand up to Stalin and communism. The right had failed to drive home their charge that he had 'lost' eastern and south-eastern Europe to the communists. Berlin had demonstrated that Stalin would be circumspect in future about challenging American power. West Europeans, happy with Marshall Aid, wanted more than economic aid. They desired security and wanted to shelter under the American umbrella. Uncle Sam was the only one who could frighten away the big, bad Moscow wolf from their door. They began pressing for a military alliance in early 1948, and it came to fruition in April 1949 as the North Atlantic Treaty Organisation (NATO).

Stalin's response to these events was to stoke up the fires of Russian nationalism at home. A mood of xenophobia was generated by the authorities as they sought to wean Russians away from western influence. All cultural influences from the west were deemed nefarious and designed to weaken Russia's resolve to defend its culture and traditions. This also applied to scientific contacts, which were now off bounds. Successful spying (especially the acquisition of atomic bomb secrets) replaced open contacts. It also made it possible to explain why living standards were not rising as rapidly as expected and why ideological vigilance was necessary and desirable. Jews were caught in this vice as anti-Semitism waxed. After the death of Andrei Zhdanov in 1948, there were purges targeted at his Leningrad political base. In eastern Europe show trials saw many executed, especially Jews. The Stalinist leadership was making Russia and eastern Europe safe for its brand of communism. The only one who got away, Yugoslavia's Tito, remained a thorn in Moscow's flesh. The peoples of the new Russian empire were paying a heavy price for the tension between Moscow and Washington.

CHINA

The United States found Chiang Kai-shek a frustrating ally. Considerable aid had been extended to the Chinese nationalist leader to do battle with the occupying Japanese, but he preferred to keep his powder dry for his long-running battle with the Chinese communists, led by Mao Zedong, and simply avoided pitched battles with the Japanese. The Americans attempted to negotiate a *modus vivendi*

between the two Chinese leaders but Chiang believed he could rout
and destroy Mao's troops, later to be known as the People's Liberation Army. This was a fatal misjudgement and despite Chiang's great
military advantage on paper, he was soon facing disaster. When
Chiang pleaded for much more war matériel, US advisors judged that
he could not be saved. President Truman did not perceive China to be
of any strategic significance for the United States and consequently
left Chiang to his fate. The People's Republic of China was proclaimed on 1 October 1949. Mao put out feelers to the United States
but Washington looked the other way. The Truman administration
declared it would not recognise communist China, and so Mao had
no other way to turn than to Russia. Was a historic opportunity lost?
Only in 1972 did Washington change its mind and rapprochement
between China and America get under way.

US Democrats seized on Chiang's expulsion from mainland China
– he repaired to Taiwan to re-establish himself and plot his return to
the mainland – to pillory the Truman administration for the 'loss' of
China. Alger Hiss was tried, and found guilty, finally in January
1950, of passing classified information to the Russians in the late
1930s. A major role in turning up evidence from a previous decade
was played by the up and coming Congressman, Richard M. Nixon.
Anxiety was compounded by the TASS announcement in September
1949 of the explosion of a Russian atomic bomb. This took the
American military by surprise as it had expected the Russians to take
a few more years to produce a nuclear device. For some, the explanation for the rapid Soviet advance in nuclear technology was simple:
there were traitors in America who were passing on nuclear secrets.
President Truman ordered that the development of the hydrogen
bomb be speeded up. In February 1950 the British announced that an
espionage ring, headed by Klaus Fuchs, had been caught passing on
atomic secrets to the Russians. In the same month, the junior senator
from Wisconsin, Joseph McCarthy, declared dramatically that he had
evidence that the Department of State was seething with communists.
He had a list of no less than 205 Communist Party members in the
institution which shaped American foreign policy. He had no such
evidence but since his claim came at a propitious time, the American
public was willing to believe the accusation. His claims were dismissed by the Truman administration, but they were nevertheless
embarrassing. The senator's brilliant but short career had begun.

Since he could not hope for any help from America, Mao was obliged to repair to Moscow to entreat Stalin to fund the transformation of China. Stalin was not amused by Mao's victory as he

would have welcomed a divided China, with the communists dependent on him. The self-confident Mao would be difficult to influence and would bridle at being expected to kowtow to Stalin's brand of communism. When Mao came to Moscow, in December 1949, to negotiate a friendship and mutual assistance treaty, Stalin kept him waiting, to underline who was the supplicant and who was the master.

Mao wanted the earth, but in the treaty of February 1950 Stalin fobbed him off with US$300 million trade credits over five years, and charged him interest. Mao did get Stalin to promise to surrender Russia's special rights in Manchurian ports and the east Chinese railway, also in Manchuria, despite the fact that Stalin had been eyeing Manchuria and inner Mongolia. But there were concessions: the Soviets were granted economic rights in Xinjiang, and Mao had to agree to mixed companies as a way of tapping Russian technical expertise. He also asked for an atomic bomb but was turned down. As a parting gift, Stalin handed Mao his man in the Politburo of the Communist Party of China, Kao Kang, on a plate, or rather to the firing squad. Kao had been Stalin's main Chinese spy and was immediately executed. The meeting was thus a strained affair, and although tension in the relationship had already surfaced in the 1920s, Stalin's attitude ensured the development of a bitter Sino-Soviet conflict.

NSC-68

In early 1950 President Truman instructed the National Security Council to undertake a fundamental reappraisal of US Cold War policy. This document, which was only declassified in the 1970s and became known as NSC-68, had a formative influence on the way America waged the Cold War, until it was superseded by the changed environment of détente. It viewed the world as bipolar: Russian and American. The scenario it sketched was apocalyptic: Russia was 'animated by a new fanatic faith, antithetical to our own, and seeks to impose its absolute authority ... In the minds of the Soviet leaders, however, achievement of this design requires the dynamic extension of their authority and the ultimate elimination of any effective opposition to their authority ... Soviet efforts are now directed toward the domination of the Eurasian land mass' [quoted in 48 p. 96]. Kennan, proponent of 'containment', did his best to undermine this analysis. He simply did not believe that Stalin had a blueprint for the conquest of the world.

Dean Acheson, Secretary of State, disregarded this view. As a politician, he needed to seize the initiative and an open invitation was extended him in the document. Having outlined the threat, NSC-68 spelled out the solution: America was to take the lead in fashioning a viable political and economic system throughout the non-communist world, or in the terms of the document, throughout the free world. Limited wars were justified if they achieved America's objectives. The document was based on a worst case scenario for the United States. What should America now do? [48 *p. 97*]. There was no point in negotiating with Moscow as the balance of forces was such that the Russians could not be coerced into concessions. Instead America had to prepare for possible military confrontation: the hydrogen bomb had to be available for deployment by 1954, since the Russians were also capable of making one; conventional forces were to be expanded rapidly to defend US power without resorting to nuclear weapons; taxes were to be increased rapidly to pay for the expensive military establishment; American society was to be mobilised to make the necessary sacrifices to implement these goals; and strong, American-led alliances should be formed around the globe. The ultimate aim was that communism should be undermined within Russia and Russians won over to the American side.

The official mood in the US had changed dramatically. Containment – accepting that the Russians were not a long-term threat to America – now gave way to the view that communist power had to be confronted and rolled back. The average American's aversion to paying taxes, let alone increased taxes, threatened to make NSC-68 just another policy document, so the administration needed a dramatic event to make its implementation irresistible. On 25 June 1950 North Korea invaded the South. The situation was transformed: 'Korea came along and saved us' [48 *p. 98*], Acheson later admitted.

THE WAR IN KOREA

With its tradition of anti-imperialism, America favoured the emergence of independent states in east and south-east Asia. The locals would not welcome the return of their colonial masters and would fight for their independence. Would independence movements be friendly to the United States or would they fall under the influence of communists? America played its part in ensuring the Dutch did not re-establish their empire in the East Indies, and an independent, non-communist Indonesia emerged. In Indo-China the French attempted to resurrect their empire but had to contend with resistance groups which had emerged under Japanese occupation. In Japan the

Americans, having smashed the Japanese military, began to promote a vibrant market economy. Security remained firmly in the hands of Washington. The Philippines were granted independence but the Americans retained strategic military bases and helped in the suppression of a communist uprising.

The US knew little about Korea as it had been under Japanese rule from 1905 until they were driven out in 1945 by Russian and American forces. Koreans wanted to be independent and resented the new occupation. Since Korea bordered on Russia, Stalin wanted to ensure that no military threat emanated from there again. The Russians and Americans began to train Koreans in the martial arts. Separate governments were formed in 1948, and in 1949 it was decided to withdraw US troops from Korea. Although Syngman Rhee, the dictator in the South, was unpopular, and it was possible that a united communist Korea might follow American withdrawal, Washington judged that the Asian mainland was outside the American defence perimeter.

Everything pointed to American lack of interest in the inevitable Korean civil war. Stalin provided the North Koreans with offensive weapons and, in so doing, promoted the invasion of the South, but he had completely misjudged the reaction of the Americans. Korea had to be saved from communism and this provided the bandwagon that the Truman administration, the US military and the right had been waiting for. It soured relations between the superpowers and held back détente for 20 years. It also set in train an arms race which would ruin Russia and contribute to the collapse of communism in 1991. The superpower confrontation spread to all corners of the globe. Vast stockpiles of nuclear weapons, which could never be used except to destroy the planet, were built up. The Korean war stimulated a cancer which gnawed away at the vitals of the world for 40 years.

The onset of the Korean civil war was inevitable. It just happened that Kim Il-sung invaded the South before Rhee had girded his loins to invade the North. The fact that Kim Il-sung had beaten Rhee to the draw transformed the situation. A Rhee invasion of the North would almost certainly have resulted in a united, communist Korea. The Americans had abandoned Chiang Kai-shek to his fate, so presumably they would have done the same to Rhee. Some viewed Kim's invasion as aggression and it was up to the United Nations to punish aggressors; otherwise the world could sink into anarchy.

The Truman administration grasped its opportunity with both hands. Kim's invasion – it was taken for granted that he had been sent south by Stalin – was the first real test for American resolve when confronted by Russian aggression. The domino theory was favoured: if Stalin were not stopped in Korea he would advance and states would fall in succession to communism until it dominated Europe and Asia or started a Third World War. If Stalin went unchecked, US promises to resist communist aggression in Europe and Asia would turn out to be hollow. The credibility of American foreign policy was at stake; Truman would become a lame duck President. The UN Security Council voted to intervene in Korea, led by the American military. Russia absented itself during the crucial vote in the Security Council, but could have cast its veto if it had been present. Was Moscow absent in order to avoid a confrontation with Washington?

Brilliantly led by General MacArthur, UN forces routed the communists in three months. Having reached the thirty-eighth parallel, the border between North and South, should UN forces cross it, overrun the North and unite Korea under a more acceptable leader than Rhee? The Truman administration decided it should invade the North, assuming that Stalin would abandon it for fear of precipitating a Third World War. The Chinese were written off as weak and their threats of intervention discounted. There were dissenting voices in Washington, one of whom was Paul Nitze, the driving force behind NSC-68, who thought the time was not ripe to risk a war with Russia. It would be better to wait until the NSC-68 recommendations had been implemented. But Truman could not resist using the mailed fist to refute the claim that he was soft on communism.

Mao and the Chinese leadership were in a quandary. They had no direct diplomatic links with the US and relied on the *New York Times* for information on American intentions. They gained the impression that the Americans, after defeating the communists in Korea, would then turn on China. Mao wanted to avoid war with the US, but was convinced the Americans would force him into a conflict, and so decided to fight on Korean rather than Chinese soil. About 200,000 Chinese troops invaded in October, and in November UN forces had been routed and the Chinese poured across the thirty-eighth parallel. The North Koreans and Chinese took tremendous losses, partly due to American air supremacy, but the war became more and more unpopular in the United States.

All the while US military power was growing, especially in nuclear weapons, guided by NSC-68, and in late 1952 the American military perceived they could confront and defeat Russia. The generals concluded that the balance of power had moved in their direction. The fact that Russia did nothing to prevent its Chinese and Korean clients from being defeated in South Korea was taken as conclusive evidence. America came to believe that it could act aggressively in pursuit of its perceived interests.

Stalin provided military equipment to the Chinese, at prices the Chinese viewed as extortionate, but did not provide the air cover he had promised them. Moscow did not intervene itself in the conflict (which eventually claimed the lives of about 3 million persons) or threaten to extend the war into other theatres. Through excellent sources of intelligence (spies) in Washington and London, Stalin was aware that the Americans had decided against invading China and using nuclear weapons, and he was convinced that the Americans could not win a conventional war in North Korea given the vast manpower resources of China. Stalin conducted a low-risk strategy, evidenced by his reneging on the deal to supply the Chinese with air cover. He was determined to deny the Americans the opportunity to attack him.

The Korean War fuelled anti-communism in America and made it impossible to propose a balanced policy towards communist states. Policy towards China was completely reversed. The Chinese had killed tens of thousands of American boys and were now regarded as full members of Stalin's evil communist empire. There could be no question of diplomatic recognition of the Beijing regime. Some nervous Europeans worried that if the communists had attempted to unite Korea by force, might they not try the same in Germany? Measures were needed to forestall this. NATO needed more European troops and West Germany could provide them. General Dwight D. Eisenhower was appointed supreme commander of allied forces in Europe and more US divisions were to be moved to Europe. The Korean War thus led to the decision to remilitarise West Germany.

The war also transformed the fortunes of Japan, which had supplied the lion's share of the provisions required by the UN forces in Korea. A tangible reward was soon forthcoming. In September 1951, in San Francisco, a peace treaty was signed which envisaged American withdrawal in May 1952. All belligerent countries signed, except of course the Soviet Union, China, North Korea and other communist states. The US kept some military bases but Japanese security was guaranteed by Washington. Japan had joined the anti-communist club. The Philippines, Japan, Australia and New Zealand signed security pacts with Washington. In Europe, Greece and Turkey joined NATO. The Americans prepared to expand their influence in the Middle East. Russia was gradually being surrounded by states relying on the United States for their security and the outlook seemed bleak for Stalin. Instead of devoting resources to vitally needed reconstruction and development at home, he was being forced to invest more and more in security [6; 9 *pp. 58–80*; 12; 48 *pp. 99–145*].

3 TO THE BRINK AND BACK: 1953–1969

THE SEARCH FOR A NEW RELATIONSHIP

Stalin died on 5 March 1953. The people mourned but some in the leadership, especially Lavrenty Beria, celebrated. Stalin's last years had been replete with suspicion and fear. At the 19th Party Congress, in October 1952, there was a call for vigilance in the face of the 'threat of a new war'. The Politburo was replaced by a Presidium, with twice as many members as the old Politburo. Was Stalin preparing a purge of the old guard so as to clear the way for a new, young, Stalin-dedicated cohort?

Tension was heightened in January 1953 when *Pravda* announced the discovery of a Doctors' Plot. Over the years since 1945 several prominent politicians had already been murdered by a group of doctors, most of whom were supposedly linked to a Jewish organisation run by the Americans. One of the accused confessed that he had received orders to 'eliminate the leading cadres of the Soviet Union'. This included comrade Stalin. The newspaper assured its readers that documentary evidence, conclusively proving the case, was available. Ministries were accused of slackness and the party and Komsomol of lacking vigilance. Then suddenly, on 23 February, the whole campaign was dropped. Shortly after Stalin's death, the so-called Plot was acknowledged as a fabrication and the Deputy Minister of State Security was blamed and shot.

A collective leadership of Malenkov, Molotov and Beria would 'prevent any kind of disorder or panic'. They hastened to relax tension at home and abroad, which was of imperative importance during the domestic power struggle. Georgy Malenkov had already called for peaceful coexistence in 1952. He now promised the Russian population a better life. Internationally, he reiterated his offer of peaceful coexistence and held out the olive branch to Tito and sent soothing words to countries bordering on the Soviet Union. Beria also launched a few initiatives. He proposed the promotion of non-Russians (he was a Georgian himself) in non-Russian republics and the unification of Germany as a neutral state. The uprising in East Berlin and Beria's arrest, both in June 1953, removed him from the scene. An intriguing question remains: had he become dominant in Moscow, would Germany have been reunited and the situation in eastern Europe transformed? In retrospect, this would have served Russia better than a divided Germany and an accelerated arms race.

KHRUSHCHEV TAKES OVER

Stalin had been cautious and keen to reduce risk to a minimum in his foreign policy. He was extremely well informed about the policies and intentions of his capitalist adversaries through his highly successful spy network, although it is not yet clear how much of this excellent reporting he believed. As a Marxist, he expected the capitalist world to sink into crisis, and the socialist world to remain outside these conflicts and then benefit from them. Khrushchev was a man of quite a different mould. He was a risk-taker in foreign affairs as he believed that Soviet socialism would eventually prevail everywhere. He also had the atomic bomb, and in August 1953 the hydrogen bomb. Russian rocketry was developing fast and there was a huge Russian scientific community servicing military ends. Khrushchev was made Party leader in September 1953 and forced Malenkov to resign as Prime Minister in February 1955.

Khrushchev's knowledge of the outside world had been garnered as a rising star under Stalin. He was a frequent guest at Stalin's home and his memoirs reveal a reasonable understanding of world politics. Of course, he suffered from the besetting sin of Russian leaders: arrogance towards other socialist states. He, like Stalin, expected their leaders to defer to him. He quickly found out that the Chinese and Yugoslavs had no intention of acknowledging his precedence. His confrontation with the Chinese was eventually to split the world communist movement and then provoke border skirmishes with Beijing.

The demise of Stalin and the change of President in America made it possible to negotiate an armistice agreement in Korea, along the thirty-eighth parallel, the *status quo ante,* on 27 July 1953. During the struggle for primacy with Malenkov, Khrushchev could not visit any leading capitalist state as head of a delegation. That was the prerogative of the Prime Minister, Malenkov, and the Foreign Minister, Molotov. Instead he could lead a delegation to any socialist state as relations with these countries came under the Communist Party.

Relations with them were fraternal, not foreign. His first stab at diplomacy was therefore in Beijing, in September 1954, when Molotov, much to his chagrin, was left at home. Mao enjoyed playing cat and mouse with Khrushchev, who found some of Mao's statements to be opaque, others so mundane as to be blindingly obvious. There was little respect on either side. Mao thought that he was the natural successor to Stalin as the leader of the communist world, but such an idea was deeply offensive to Khrushchev. Mao got the better of the exchanges: the Russians gave up their Chinese ports and dissolved their joint-stock companies. Mao even asked for Outer Mongolia (the Mongolian People's Republic, Chinese until 1911) but was put in his place.

In May 1955 Khrushchev and company made for Belgrade to bring Yugoslavia back into the Russian fold. Again Molotov was left at home. Khrushchev blamed all the misunderstandings during the years since 1948, when Yugoslavia had been expelled from the Cominform, on Beria, but Tito was not taken in. Only in 1956 could comrade Stalin be blamed for his policy mistakes. Khrushchev wanted to restore inter-party relations, in other words the Yugoslavs were to recognise the leadership of the Communist Party of the Soviet Union, but Tito would not bite and offered instead to restore inter-state relations.

Russia was seeking to mend all its fences with the outside world. It was mindful of the need to restrict its military budget so as to strengthen its economy and raise living standards. It wanted peace with everyone. Nuclear weapons promised to make it possible to cut the defence budget, but would the Americans play ball? There was precious little trust between the two superpowers [*Doc. 1*]. No successful agreement had been negotiated during the Cold War so far, and a major problem for both sides was lack of knowledge of the other. It would take until the Gorbachev era before both sides could feel completely comfortable with one another.

When Stalin died there was a new President in the White House, General Dwight Eisenhower, and a new Secretary of State, John Foster Dulles: Eisenhower was a war hero and had served as NATO Commander-in-Chief; Dulles was steeped in foreign affairs and had served under Truman. The presidential campaign had been dirty. Eisenhower's Vice-President was Richard Nixon, skilled at muckraking. Joseph McCarthy campaigned for Eisenhower and dragged George Marshall's name in the mud. He and all his ilk, McCarthy claimed, had betrayed America, refusing to stand up to the communists. Dulles called the containment policy 'immoral' and spoke of the 'liberation of captive nations' and the roll-back of communism in eastern Europe and east Asia. The American right was on a roll.

Fortunately for America, Eisenhower and Dulles were level-headed, cautious and reasonable. The vast increase in defence spending in the early 1950s increased self-confidence and Eisenhower was able to quieten those in the military who advocated a pre-emptive strike against the Russians. Apprehensive about the growth of what he termed the 'military-industrial complex', in the United States, he wanted to reduce military spending and eventually balance the budget. Eisenhower chose to concentrate on air and nuclear power. The Americans might use nuclear weapons to counter a Russian conventional attack and Dulles spoke of 'massive retaliation' at the slightest provocation. Despite this rhetoric, Eisenhower was keen to reduce the risk of nuclear war.

Russian policy in Europe centred on Germany and the aim was to ensure that Germany did not rearm and become a threat. Until 1955, Austrian and German policy went hand in hand. The goal was to create unified, neutral states, but all Moscow's blandishments in Germany came to nothing as the west feared that a united, neutral Germany might slide into the Russian orbit. In May 1955 Moscow decided to separate the two states and accept a united, neutral Austria. The Austrian peace treaty was signed by the four occupying powers or Big Four (America, Russia, Britain and France) and resulted in the withdrawal of all foreign troops. This was the first instance that Russian soldiers had voluntarily left a country they had occupied in 1945. There was a bonus for Moscow: NATO could no longer use Austria as a link between West Germany and Italy. The occupation of West Germany came to an end and it joined NATO, also in May 1955. The GDR was admitted to the Warsaw Pact, the Russian response to NATO.

THE GENEVA SUMMIT

Despite this, the Big Four agreed to meet in Geneva in July 1955 to discuss nuclear weapons and the German question. Eisenhower put forward what later became known as the 'open skies' proposal. He suggested each side provide the other with a list of its military installations and that aerial reconnaissance be permitted to check that no attack was imminent. Khrushchev backed off, but when he offered partial reconnaissance two years later it was the Americans who backed off. At Geneva, the two leaders agreed on a moratorium on nuclear testing, without, of course, permitting any verification.

Nevertheless it was a landmark: the two sides were talking to one another constructively, for the first time since 1945. After the flat beer of the previous years, the Geneva spirit was quite inebriating. On Germany, Khrushchev talked about all-German elections. On his way home, though, he dropped in on Walter Ulbricht, the GDR leader, in East Berlin and assured him that the 'socialist achievements' of the GDR would be preserved. In other words, Moscow, for the first time, formally gave up its dream of a united Germany. Khrushchev had decided that increasing trade with West Germany came before everything else. Konrad Adenauer was invited to Moscow in September 1955, and diplomatic relations were established. He tried to 'buy' the GDR by offering generous credits and reparations but Khrushchev resisted the temptation. The Russians had to accept a divided Germany and a divided Europe – for the time being.

In February 1956 Khrushchev shocked communists and non-communists alike by denouncing Stalin. The self-confident Party leader declared that peaceful co-existence was the basis of relations with the capitalist world. This, however, did not mean that Moscow accepted a static world order. The class struggle, between the oppressed and the oppressors world-wide, would continue. There would be no peaceful co-existence as far as ideology was concerned. In April 1956 the Cominform was dissolved. This was one of the preconditions which Tito demanded for the normalisation of relations. Its activities were transferred to the Central Committee Secretariat and a department for liaison with communist and workers' parties was eventually set up.

THE HUNGARIAN REVOLUTION

Khrushchev's rapprochement with Tito and his declaration that there were national roads to communism fuelled hopes in eastern Europe that Russian control might be loosened. This was particularly so in Poland and Hungary. Eventually the Poles forced the Russians to accept their choice of leader, Gomulka, in October. No resolution to the tension in Hungary could be brokered, however. On 23 October police fired on a peaceful demonstration which was demanding the return to power of Imre Nagy, the former Prime Minister. The revolution was under way. Nagy was appointed Prime Minister and on 1 November declared that Hungary had left the Warsaw Pact and called on the UN to recognise Hungary as a neutral state.

Khrushchev and the Russian leadership were in a quandary about whether to intervene or not. On 28 October, and again on 30 October, the Presidium (Politburo) resolved to seek a peaceful solution by withdrawing the Russian army. But on 31 October this decision was reversed and Moscow chose the military option. The reason for the change of mind appears to have been strong Chinese support for the military option. Tito also favoured using force. Another reason for the intervention was Khrushchev's fear that if he abandoned the Hungarian comrades (and Nasser during the Suez conflict which was being fought out at the same time), the decision could split the Presidium and, possibly, lead to his removal. Despite strong oral American support for the Hungarians, the United States was not willing to risk a Third World War by intervening militarily.

ASIA

There were also serious tensions in Asia. The French were determined to stay in Indo-China but the Viet Minh communists, led by Ho Chi Minh, were equally determined to defeat and expel them from the region. The guerrilla tactics of the Viet Minh were proving successful and, far from home, the French found it ever more difficult to provision the existing troops and provide fresh ones for the conflict. In France there was political instability and governments changed often, rendering a coherent colonial policy in south-east Asia more difficult. There was also the burgeoning financial burden which France was ill-equipped to bear. The war went badly until, facing disaster at Dien Bien Phu in March 1954, the French were obliged to call for American intervention. In 1954 the Americans were paying about 70 per cent of the French military budget and had advisers in Indo-China. Eisenhower and Dulles feared that if the French were defeated, the whole of Indo-China would fall to the communists. The same might happen in Malaya, Indonesia, Taiwan and South Korea. A US general recommended the use of a few small, atomic bombs. Sir Winston Churchill refused to come to France's aid, seeing it as a lost cause.

The American military did not want another Korea with their men dying on foreign fields. If the US intervened, would China also come in? In the event, the French surrendered and a new government in Paris negotiated peace in Indo-China: Ho Chi Minh controlled about two-thirds of Vietnam but agreed to withdraw north of the seventeenth parallel; and there were to be national elections within two years to unify the country. The pro-communist Pathet Lao forces were given free rein in Laos and there were to be national elections in Cambodia. Ho concentrated on reconstructing North Vietnam, with Russian assistance. He was certain to win the national elections. The US was not a party to the peace agreement and refused to acknowledge it. Given the anti-communist mood in America, Eisenhower and Dulles deemed it wise not to concede communist control over North Vietnam. The Americans decided to channel their aid directly to the South Vietnamese, cutting out the French. They began training a South Vietnamese army. In July 1955, with most of the French gone, Diem, the American-picked head of government, announced that national elections would not take place.

Dulles believed that an alliance, similar to NATO in Europe, was needed to prevent the spread of communism in Asia, and so on 8 September 1954 the United States, France, Great Britain, Australia, New Zealand, Thailand, Pakistan and the Philippines agreed to establish the South East Asia Treaty Organisation (SEATO). South Vietnam, Laos and Cambodia were of special concern. Indonesia, India and Burma declined to join. They did not view the communist threat in the same apocalyptic terms as the Americans. American forces, Dulles assured the Senate, would only be committed when communists were clearly in the ascendancy and the Senate would approve intervention. Initial involvement would be by the air force, not the army. Significantly, the treaty provided for the deployment of American military might to prevent a communist party successfully challenging for power in a state. The other members of the alliance made clear they would not intervene in such a case. Fateful decisions had been taken.

The Taiwan problem caused Eisenhower and Dulles endless problems. The latter profoundly mistrusted Chiang Kai-shek, suspecting that he was angling to embroil the US in a conflict with China, in which Chiang could take over as ruler of China after American troops had cleared the mainland of communists. Mao was alarmed by the formation of SEATO and he thought the US was planning to separate Taiwan from the mainland. Consequently China began bombing some of the offshore islands and thought this would make the Americans wary of committing themselves to Chiang. It had the opposite effect: Washington could not be seen to be abandoning Taiwan as it would send the wrong messages throughout east and south-east Asia. A defence pact was signed with Chiang but the latter had to promise not to attack the mainland without Washington's consent. The US would also not defend the offshore islands held by Chiang.

Washington pressed Beijing to renounce the use of force to regain Taiwan but the Chinese demurred, seeing the matter as the uncompleted part of the civil war. In 1957 the Americans broke off the talks. Mao began to press Khrushchev for support for an offensive against the offshore islands Jinmen (Quemoy) and Mazu (Matsu).

The Americans threatened nuclear retaliation and the Chinese desisted. One of the reasons for the Chinese backdown was Russia's refusal to provide offensive military aid to China. They would only help if America invaded China. This caused great anger in Beijing as it became clear that the Russians would not risk a conflict with the Americans to help the Chinese.

It would not take long for the communist giants to fall out [*Doc.* 2]. According to the Chinese, the Russians, on 20 June 1959, unilaterally 'tore up the agreement on new technology' and 'refused to provide China with a sample atomic bomb and technical data concerning its manufacture'. The first Chinese-Indian border skirmish, on 9 September 1959, resulted in Moscow adopting a neutral stance, to the chagrin of the Chinese. When Khrushchev visited Beijing, on his way home from a summit with President Eisenhower, he asked for a Russia radio base to keep in touch with its submarines in the Pacific. Mao countered with a request for atomic data. Neither got anything. The festering Sino-Soviet conflict burst into public view at a Congress of the Romanian Party, in Bucharest, in June 1960. Ostensibly it was about socialism and de-Stalinisation (Mao had expected Khrushchev to consult him before debunking Stalin), but in reality it was about leadership of the communist movement and international status. Khrushchev informed the Russian public about the divorce at the 22nd Party Congress, in February 1961.

THE MIDDLE EAST

Oil made the Middle East strategically important, since about two-thirds of the oil available to the west was there. The region was overwhelmingly Arab and Muslim. When Israel was established in 1948, logically America should have supported the Arabs, but there was a powerful Jewish political lobby in America. The British and French had dominated the region in the inter-war years; after 1945, France faded away but Britain remained. It controlled Iranian oil and the Iranian government sought every opportunity to acquire control over its most important asset. When Mossadeq, the Prime Minister, nationalised the Anglo-Iranian oil company, oil exports stopped and the Iranian economy declined, and there were rumours of a Russian loan for Mossadeq. Dulles, after a visit to the region, was alarmed by the neutral stance of states in the conflict between 'slavery' and 'freedom'. The US and Britain helped the Shah to reassert himself in August 1953, and the British were forced to give up their oil monopoly. In a new consortium America and Britain obtained 40 per cent each: for the Americans it was good politics and good business. The Americans were seeking for ways to fashion an alliance system in the Middle East to prevent Russian expansion but always ran up against the problem of Israel. Washington was perceived by Arab states as siding with the Israelis against the Palestinians, indeed as taking the Jewish side in the Arab-Israeli conflict. The Jewish lobby in Washington was strong and US Jews also channelled financial aid to Israel. Israel was, however, America's main ally in the Middle East. Eventually, in February 1956, Turkey and Iraq signed what later became known as the Baghdad Pact, and Great Britain, Pakistan and Iran joined later the same year. The United States never joined. The pact antagonised those Arabs, first and foremost Egypt's Nasser, who believed the region should not become involved in the Cold War.

The Americans wanted to step into the vacuum left by the exit of the British from Egypt but Nasser was calling for Arab socialism and war against Israel. Russia was also keen to step into the vacuum and Czechoslovak arms were soon on their way to Cairo. Nasser had proved he could play off east against west. But he came unstuck when arranging finance to construct the Aswan dam, to provide irrigation water and power. The Americans backed out and Nasser nationalised the Suez canal, run by an Anglo-French company, to raise funds. Anthony Eden (later Lord Avon), the British Prime Minister, overreacted, seeing Nasser as another Hitler who could only be stopped with force. France, Israel and Britain secretly co-ordinated war plans and on 29 October 1956, while Khrushchev was agonising in Moscow over the Russian response to the Hungarian revolution, they struck against Egypt.

What was the US to do? Traditionally an anti-imperialist power, could Washington side with its allies and alienate the Arabs? Eisenhower and Dulles decided that their long-term goals in the Middle East came first and sided with Russia in the United Nations. The war was to end and the belligerents to go home. Khrushchev, secure in the knowledge that the Americans would not come to the aid of the British and French, threatened them with nuclear missiles if they did not go home. It was the end of British and French power in the Middle East and also Eden's political career. He had made the fatal mistake of assuming the Americans would remain neutral.

Afterwards, Congress declared the Middle East a region of vital national interest and the President could come to the aid of any state under threat. It became known as the Eisenhower doctrine. In 1957, when King Hussein of Jordan felt threatened by pro-Nasser forces in his country, the Americans stepped in and he received US$10 million in aid. It paid to be America's friend. In 1958 American marines landed in Lebanon to help the President against pro-Nasser opponents. In Iraq, the pro-western king and government were overthrown and a nationalist, anti-western regime took over. Khrushchev threatened to intervene militarily if the Americans did not leave, but Washington left when it decided Arab nationalism would not sell out to Moscow.

OTHER THIRD WORLD STATES

Khrushchev was looking for ways of establishing contact with Asian Third World states in order to counter American influence. The Bandung conference of Afro-Asian states, in Bandung, Indonesia, condemned racism and colonialism. This was a breakthrough for the Russian leader and he was attracted by its anti-western credentials. In November–December 1955 he and Prime Minister Bulganin visited India, where the crowds were so great they were almost crushed to death, as well as Burma and Afghanistan. President Sukarno of Indonesia was invited to Moscow and promised arms and technical assistance. Communists in Indonesia supported him and made Dulles nervous. Washington provided assistance and aid but Sukarno was very ambitious and played east off against west. In 1958 Eisenhower used the CIA to promote Sumatran secession as the Americans believed many island states were preferable to one Indonesia. The attempt failed but America was caught red-handed. Khrushchev beamed and increased military aid.

Khrushchev's first foray into black Africa was in the Republic of the Congo, the former Belgian Congo, where Patrice Lumumba became the Prime Minister on independence in June 1960. Mineral resources, especially copper, in Katanga province proved too valuable to abandon and the Belgians promoted its secession. Lumumba appealed to the US, the UN and Russia to help reunify the country, and the UN passed a resolution appealing to the Belgians to leave and granting military assistance for Lumumba. Nothing happened, confirming the rule that the UN only deploys troops when the US is in favour. The Congo was a long way away and of little interest.

Lumumba appealed again to Moscow. This time, Khrushchev jumped in and sent military equipment and technicians. This sent alarm bells ringing in Washington and UN troops flew in. There was a risk that the Congo could go communist and begin a chain reaction in the region. The CIA considered assassinating Lumumba but he was dismissed from office in September 1960. He then attempted a coup but UN forces closed Kinshasa airport and prevented the Russians airlifting in pro-Lumumba forces. He was replaced by Joseph Mobotu, acceptable to the Americans (until eventually forced into exile in 1997). Lumumba was killed in 1961and became a hero in the Soviet bloc. A university for Third World students, in Moscow, was named after him. When the cards were down, far from home, the Americans could always beat the Russians. Khrushchev could rant and rave, in the UN and elsewhere, against American imperialism and threaten them with his missiles. All he achieved was the acceleration of the arms race [9 *pp. 85–120*; 11 *pp. 121–42*; 42; 48 *pp. 146–94*; 50; 56].

BRINKMANSHIP: BERLIN

The space age was launched on 4 October 1957 when Sputnik circumnavigated the globe every 96 minutes. It was a staggering achievement for Russian science to propel an 83.6 kg satellite into space for three months. Then it returned to the earth's atmosphere and burned out. However, it was not a bolt from the blue. It was followed by another eight Sputniks which scored a dazzling list of firsts, the first dog in space, and so on. Russian rocket technology was the best in the world and threatened to alter the balance of world power. Khrushchev exulted and Russians felt proud. They had put one over on the Americans. As events were to show, Khrushchev became dangerously over-confident. Everything was not as it seemed. Eisenhower had actually prevented America from being the first in space. The capacity had been there but the US President was concerned about sending a space vehicle over enemy territory. He wanted the Russians to go first and then the Americans would follow. Had the US gone first, it might have lowered the tension of the ensuing five years.

Convinced he had secured the upper hand in missiles, Khrushchev resolved to push America to the limit. He was riding high after successfully seeing off the Anti-Party group which had attempted to remove him in June 1957. He then became a strong, national leader. The Prime Minister, Marshal Bulganin, had sided with the losers and was left in power for appearance's sake. As the Yugoslav ambassador, Micunovic, remarked to Khrushchev, it would not be advisable to give the impression that he had become Stalin mark II. In early 1958 Khrushchev pushed Bulganin aside and became Prime Minister himself. He was the supreme decision-maker until the Cuban missile crisis of 1962 weakened him, when his opponents began to plot his downfall.

Berlin was the west's Achilles' heel. Khrushchev, in his down-to-earth language, called it the west's 'balls'. Every 'time I squeeze them, the west squeals'. Rustic but right. West Germany was now a member of NATO and the Russians were concerned that Bonn might acquire access to nuclear weapons, since it was provided with nuclear-capable artillery and fighter bombers. The US was building up tactical (short-range) nuclear weapons and ballistic missiles which could reach the Soviet Union. They were intended to counter Russia's superiority in conventional (non-nuclear) forces. In 1958 NATO thought of providing West Germany with 'defensive' nuclear weapons [*39 p. 94*].

As a strong, national leader, Khrushchev had three goals: ensure the economy expanded as rapidly as possible; increase Russia's security; and expand communism throughout the world. Russia's security held the key. The greater defence spending, the less investment there would be for the civilian economy and for raising living standards. Rocket superiority promised a solution. Perhaps the US could be forced into disarmament negotiations and rockets could replace some ground forces in Russia.

The Berlin crisis of 1958–62 was provoked by Khrushchev. It is still not clear, from the archives, whether Khrushchev had a grand plan to force the west out of West Berlin, gradually allow the GDR to take over, transfer Moscow's occupation rights to the GDR and oblige the west to conclude, together with the Soviet Union, a peace treaty with both German states. What is clear is that Khrushchev accepted Ulbricht's point that if the open boundary with West Berlin were not closed, the GDR would not achieve its economic potential. Workers, scientists and other professionals could simply vote with their feet if they thought the sacrifices being demanded of them were too great. It is not clear why Khrushchev launched his ultimatum in November 1958, and why then. It is also not possible to state if Ulbricht first suggested the démarche to Khrushchev. Many commentators see Khrushchev as acting impulsively without having thought through the full consequences of his action. The Soviet side did understand that one of the options the United States might choose was to go to war. Khrushchev read Adenauer's statement, in March 1958, that an 'Austrian solution' (unified, neutral state) to the German question was acceptable to him, as a sign of the increasing weakness of the west. During the Berlin crisis, the GDR consistently argued for a vigorous, confrontational pose.

On 27 November 1958 the Soviet Union issued its first Berlin ultimatum. All Russian rights in Berlin were to be transferred to the

GDR. Within six months, West Berlin was to become an 'independent, political entity, a free city'. If no such agreement were reached, the allies' access to West Berlin would be regulated by the GDR. The allies replied, on 31 December, that they regarded the previous arrangements as still in force and refused to negotiate with the GDR authorities (the west did not recognise the GDR in international law). Khrushchev warned the US that if it used force in Berlin, a Third World War would result. Recognition of the GDR and the prevention of West German access to nuclear weapons were some of the goals being pursued by the Russian leadership. Talks were held in Geneva in the summer of 1959, but no progress was made. The Russians reiterated, on numerous occasions, their demand that West Berlin become a 'demilitarised, free city' [30].

Khrushchev had always been fascinated by America and sought an invitation to visit his main adversary. The Americans thought that by inviting him he would become more amenable to a Berlin settlement which would end confrontation. In September 1959 he became the first Soviet leader to visit the US. Talks at Camp David with President Eisenhower papered over some of the cracks and Khrushchev withdrew his Berlin ultimatum. The greatest disappointment for Khrushchev was that his ardent desire to visit Disneyland was frustrated – the Americans said they could not guarantee his safety.

The west did not budge on Berlin but Khrushchev was sanguine that the problem could be resolved at the Paris summit in May 1960. Bonn was strongly against any concessions on Berlin. By early 1960 US spy planes had confirmed that Khrushchev's talk of intercontinental ballistic missile (ICBM) superiority was nothing but Russian *vrane* (boastful lies). On 1 May 1960 the Russians announced the downing of a U2 spy plane, with pilot Gary Powers taken alive, near Sverdlovsk (now Ekaterinburg). This confirmed that Russian missiles had become more effective but it also demonstrated to Khrushchev that the Americans knew he was engaging in missile bluff. He torpedoed the Paris summit of the Big Four (Russia, America, Britain and France), on European security, by demanding that Eisenhower personally apologise for the U2 incident. Khrushchev had gained the upper hand diplomatically by contradicting Eisenhower's statement that no spy plane had been flying over the Urals. He showed photographs and revealed that the pilot had been captured alive. The British Prime Minister, Harold Macmillan, pointed out to Khrushchev that it was unrealistic to expect the President of the US to apologise in such a humiliating situation. A major reason for

Khrushchev's action appears to have been the rapidly deteriorating relationship with China. Mao opposed a rapprochement with the west and advocated aggressive nuclear diplomacy, so Khrushchev's belligerence may have been partly designed to reassure him.

In the Berlin crisis, Khrushchev informed Ulbricht on 30 November 1960 that, in order to protect the prestige of the Soviet Union, his threat of concluding a separate peace treaty with the GDR would have to be made good. Ulbricht objected that this might lead to a trade boycott by the West Germans which would cripple the GDR. Khrushchev countered, without making any calculations, that the Soviet Union would make up the deficit (later it proved incapable of doing this). Ulbricht was now in a no-lose situation and could always counsel confrontation. In a letter to Khrushchev, on 18 January 1961, Ulbricht requested a Warsaw Pact conference to strengthen the position of the GDR and to force the west to make concessions on Berlin. The increasing flow of refugees to West Berlin was making these more urgent. Khrushchev replied that he wanted first to discuss the matter with Kennedy. If the President did not make any concessions, Khrushchev would discuss the implementation of their agreed measures with Ulbricht. The Warsaw Pact conference took place on 28–29 March 1961 but no one was willing to agree to the full GDR demands. Khrushchev concluded that Yury Gagarin's first flight in space, in April 1961, and the Bay of Pigs disaster, in May 1961, had weakened Kennedy [31].

Khrushchev met the new American President John F. Kennedy in Vienna in June 1961, and thought he had taken his measure. Kennedy made it clear that he did not want war but would not concede on Berlin. Khrushchev responded that if war were to come, it should come sooner rather than later, when the weapons would be even more terrifying. Kennedy did not take Khrushchev's outburst about war all that seriously. The Russian leader judged that the young American President might buckle under pressure and was soon to put him under immense pressure over Cuba.

Khrushchev then informed Ulbricht he wanted a Warsaw Pact conference as soon as possible to advance matters. At the end of June, Khrushchev permitted Ulbricht to begin making preparations to divide Berlin. Kennedy addressed the American nation on television on 25 July 1961 and underlined that the real question was not West Berlin but American credibility throughout the world. Access to West Berlin, the garrisons there and the viability of the city would be defended. The President, however, did not state that access from West to East Berlin would be defended. Here was a way out for

Moscow. Khrushchev's first reaction to the speech was to declare that it was a declaration of war, but he soon calmed down.

The Warsaw Pact summit on 3–5 August decided to divide the city, initially with barbed wire, and then, if the west did not react, with a wall. This was all the GDR would be permitted to undertake, it was not to move a 'millimeter beyond this'. The GDR was not to prevent western military personnel entering East Berlin since this would have led to Soviet personnel being barred from West Berlin. On 13 August 1961 West Berlin was completely sealed off from East Berlin and the GDR. The west did not intervene. Kennedy and Khrushchev were both relieved.

On 15 September Ulbricht wrote to Khrushchev informing him that he was drafting a peace treaty. Khrushchev, in his reply, on 28 September, failed to mention the peace treaty. Khrushchev and Ulbricht did not give up. In February and March 1962 Soviet military aircraft interfered with traffic in the air corridors to West Berlin and the west began to fear that the land routes would be blocked. Just why these moves occurred is not clear, nor are the reasons why Moscow suddenly backed off. In September 1962 the Russians stopped a US military convoy en route to West Berlin. The Americans warned Moscow they would not take this lying down. Again the Russians backed down. The GDR, in January 1963, dropped all mention of West Berlin and a separate treaty and began to propose a confederation with West Germany. This was not the end of the matter. Again in October–November 1963 the Russians halted US military convoys but after protests allowed them to proceed.

It appeared that if the west were resolute, it could outstare Khrushchev. His diplomacy consisted of an eclectic mix of threats and calls for negotiations. This made him unpredictable and, consequently, not a leader one could trust. The Americans, predictably, concluded that the best policy was to negotiate from strength. Afterwards when tension increased over Berlin, talks always defused the tension. In 1969 Andrei Gromyko signalled that the Soviet Union desired to negotiate a Berlin agreement with America, Britain and France, and this led to the Quadripartite agreement of 3 September 1971. The recognition of the GDR by the west and West Germany followed and the Berlin issue ceased to be peace-threatening [3; 31; 73].

BRINKMANSHIP: CUBA

Superpower brinkmanship on Berlin consisted in the west repeatedly making clear that its position in Berlin was non-negotiable and the

Soviet Union trying initiative after initiative to force concessions. America was asking for nothing but to be left alone. It was Moscow which was trying to change the balance. But the Berlin crisis rarely threatened to escalate into a Third World War. Cuba, however, was quite different and brought the world very close to nuclear war [*Doc. 4*]. Brinkmanship almost tipped over the edge. There, America was attempting to get Moscow to remove its medium-range nuclear missiles by escalating its threats. In Cuba, the United States was, once more, the status quo power wishing to revert to a pre-crisis situation. The Soviet Union, again, was attempting to change the strategic balance.

At the Bay of Pigs in April 1961, Cuban exiles supported by the CIA failed ignominiously to overthrow Fidel Castro. However, it was a self-inflicted disaster as the President was mainly to blame. The Joint Chiefs of Staff informed him that the mission by 1,500 Cubans to overthrow Castro had 'little chance of success'. This assessment was repeated on several occasions. The President chose to back the CIA, which was very optimistic that the Cubans, trained by them, would succeed. He personally took the decision to move the invasion from the east coast to the swampy Bay of Pigs on the southern coast, and also to reduce cover from the air force and navy. The whole episode was a disaster as 300 Cubans were killed and 1,179 captured. A humiliated Kennedy was forced to negotiate with Castro and it took 20 months and a ransom of US$53 million, paid in baby food, medicine and medical equipment, to get them released. There was now the danger that Kennedy would again try to topple Castro. At the 22nd Party Congress, Marshal Malinovsky, the Minister of Defence, reiterated Soviet claims to military superiority.

On 30 November President Kennedy authorised Operation Mongoose, to 'help Cuba overthrow the communist regime'. Fidel's Cubans infiltrated the CIA and obtained a document which stated that if Castro had not gone by October 1962, tougher measures would have to be taken. Robert McNamara, Defence Secretary, ordered that preparations be made so as to make the invasion of Cuba by 20 October possible. The US had conclusive proof that the Russians were building missile sites on Cuba, and on 22 October warned Khrushchev that an attack from Cuba would be construed by America as an attack by the Soviet Union. A quarantine was imposed to prevent any more missiles being shipped to Cuba – in reality they were already all in place.

There were 42,000 Russian troops on Cuba, armed with tactical nuclear weapons, at the disposal of local Russian commanders. The

Russians speeded up the construction of missile sites. A showdown was approaching. On 25 October Russian ships making for Cuba were turned back. The US made it clear it would attack before the missile sites became operational. Plans for an air strike on 29 or 30 October were in full swing. On 26 October Khrushchev cabled Kennedy expressing his readiness to negotiate. The same evening, Robert Kennedy met Anatoly Dobrynin, who informed him that the removal of American missiles in Turkey might contribute to the resolution of the conflict. The President stated that he expected the missiles to go after the crisis. (This meeting was kept secret for over 25 years.) On 28 October Khrushchev announced that he had ordered the dismantling of the offensive weapons and their shipment back to Russia. The Americans declined formally to promise that they would never invade Cuba but informally kept to this understanding. American Jupiter missiles were to be removed from Turkey (only revealed to the American public in 1968). The Russian leader felt humiliated but he had chosen peace, not war [3; 9 *pp. 131–44*; 19; 58; 59].

The shock of the crisis transformed Russian-American relations. A hotline was put in place as a result of the difficulty of direct contact between the two leaders. There was also now a desire to avoid confrontation and for détente. From now on, conflict was transferred to the Third World, to Vietnam, Ethiopia, Somalia, Angola, Mozambique, Afghanistan and elsewhere. It led to defeat for America in Vietnam and Russia in Afghanistan. No one gained from these conflicts, everyone was the poorer for them. The need to intervene was fuelled by the zero sum mentality: if the opposition gains ascendancy in a state, then the other is the loser. Only Gorbachev was brave enough to break this vicious circle.

THE WAR IN VIETNAM

The Americans came to regard Indo-China as indispensable for their security [*Doc. 3*]. The region must not be allowed to go communist, otherwise communism might become unstoppable in south-east and south Asia. Vietnam north of the seventeenth parallel was conceded to the communists but everything else had to be held. Eisenhower did not want to become the President who had 'lost' Indo-China. Kennedy shared these views. However, he took a relaxed view of Laos, and eventually America recognised it as neutral, even though pro-communist forces were in the ascendancy.

Vietnam was quite a different matter. No Democrat could win the presidential election in 1964 if Vietnam went red. Kennedy increased the number of US military advisers and permitted them to engage in combat; they could use napalm and defoliate the forests. Then combat troops began trickling in. There were over 16,000 by the time Kennedy was assassinated in November 1963. The Americans deluded themselves into believing they could defeat the communists by military force, but the real battle in South Vietnam was political, economic and social. Unless the Diem regime offered something superior to communism, it would lose.

Generals vied with one another for ascendancy and Washington was happy to choose the leader. However, in 1964 the leader had no political base among the people. When the North Vietnamese attacked a US destroyer in the Gulf of Tonkin in August 1964, President Johnson was presented with a pretext to bomb the North. Congress empowered the President to use whatever force he deemed necessary to resist communism in south-east Asia.

Bombing of North Vietnam began in February 1965. This gave birth to the protest movement as more and more Americans became alarmed at the extension of the war. The US had become embroiled in a war without a debate in America or any declaration of war. World-wide, America was being perceived as an aggressor, imposing its will on poor, underdeveloped Vietnam. In 1968 most Americans thought the war a mistake.

In May 1968 Washington and Hanoi began peace talks, and in October Johnson called off the bombing of the North. The Russians had applied pressure on the North Vietnamese (they provided the lion's share of their war equipment) and the US forced the South Vietnamese into line. Now the struggle was to concentrate on who should rule South Vietnam.

Nixon was elected President at this point, and promised to end the war, but he did not want to become the first American President to admit military defeat. In May 1970 the US invaded neutral Cambodia, determined to eliminate North Vietnamese supply routes to the South. The unfortunate result was that a murderous civil war ensued, with Pol Pot and the Khmer Rouge the eventual victors. In February 1971 South Vietnamese forces, supported by US air power, extended the war to Laos, again with disastrous results. As the Soviet Union and China were keen on improving relations with the US, Hanoi had to accept a peace settlement in late 1972. The South refused to accept it and the war continued with the US engaging in massive bombing of the North.

Nixon and the US got out in February 1973, providing the South with enormous amounts of war matériel. The final offensive occurred

in March 1975 when Saigon fell to the communists and became Ho
Chi Minh City. By then Nixon had left the White House, a victim of
Watergate. Promises he had made to the South Vietnamese government went with him. Vietnam was a disaster of epic proportions for
the Americans. It undermined the economy, the legitimacy of government, belief in the rightness of the nation's cause and divided the
country. However, it made American policy-makers more cautious
about the use of force world-wide. The huge budget deficits run up
during the war undermined the dollar and it eventually came off the
gold standard. Other countries, such as Japan, seized their chance.
Not until the 1990s would America recover its economic health and
re-establish itself as the world's most powerful economy [9 *pp. 156–
81*; 27; 38].

The Americans did have some luck in south-east Asia. In 1965 the
Indonesian Communist Party (PKI), with 3 million members in a
population of around 100 million, appeared to be challenging for
power, aided by the Chinese. An anti-Chinese, anti-communist coup
by the right destroyed the party and with it the threat that Indonesia,
of key strategic significance in the region, would change sides or even
become a communist state. Had Indonesia gone communist, at a time
when US intervention was increasing in Vietnam, it might have al-
tered the strategic balance significantly in Indo-China. The defeat of
the PKI protected America's flank from attack.

4 DETENTE: 1969–1979

FORGING A NEW RELATIONSHIP

When Khrushchev was removed in October 1964, he was not criticised for the direction of his foreign policy, only the means he had used. Aleksei Kosygin, the Prime Minister, took the lead in diplomacy. A cautious man, a technocrat, he was more concerned about increasing the efficiency of the domestic economy than taking risks abroad. Relations with the Chinese became more polite after Khrushchev's passing but the two leading communist powers did not come closer together.

In Hanoi, in February 1965, Kosygin counselled caution, a negotiated settlement and a long-term approach to winning control of the South. While he was there, the Americans bombed the North for the first time. The Soviet Union had to step up military deliveries. This pleased China, which would have welcomed a Russian-American nuclear confrontation. By then, however, China had succumbed to the cultural revolution, beginning in 1966. Mao had launched it in the belief that the existing elites were becoming too conservative and resistant to his leadership. The mayhem weakened China over the next decade and an era came to an end with Mao's death in 1976. The Arab-Israeli war in June 1967 found the two superpowers on opposite sides.

Kosygin was invited to meet President Johnson, at Glassboro', New Jersey, just after the end of the war. When the Russians received the invitation, they looked for but could not find Glassboro' on any of their maps and began to think that the invitation was a hoax! To overcome their embarrassing ignorance of America, they decided to establish what became known as the US and Canada Institute, Academy of Sciences. Glassboro' was the only summit between America and Russia between 1961 and 1972. The two leaders discussed the Middle East and Vietnam but no progress was made. Nevertheless, Johnson accepted a return invitation to visit Moscow.

Then came Czechoslovakia where the Prague 'spring' had given a new meaning to democratic socialism. The Czechoslovaks were edging towards social democracy but their new leader, Alexander Dubcek, did not appreciate that his espousal of greater democracy in Czechoslovakia was perceived as a threat to socialist orthodoxy in Moscow. Tension increased and Moscow enquired about the American view on the situation. President Johnson informed the Soviets that the US would not intervene in what he considered an intra-communist polemic. The Warsaw Pact invasion of Czechoslovakia was therefore free to go ahead in August 1968, fatally weakening the communist movement. West European parties, led by the Italians, sided with the Czechoslovak reform communists and condemned Russian intervention. For a brief time, Eurocommunism, the democratic face of communism, flourished in western Europe. The invasion ended hopes for greater autonomy for enterprises in the Soviet Union and the slow decline of the Soviet economy set in. The Chinese vented their anger on what they perceived to be social imperialism. This masked the apprehension that Russia might decide to intervene in China. The Brezhnev doctrine was born which obliged socialist states to intervene in one another's affairs if socialism were perceived to be in danger. Who decided when socialism was in danger? Russia, of course. This in turn led to the fateful decision to intervene in Afghanistan in December 1979. It would be left to Gorbachev to extricate the Soviet Union from its expensive blunders. In June 1969 a conference of communist and workers' parties convened but the Chinese, North Vietnamese and North Koreans declined to attend. There was no world communist movement any more.

A NEW PRESIDENT AND A NEW APPROACH

The arrival of Richard Nixon in the White House in 1969, and his choice of Henry Kissinger as head of the National Security Council until 1975, and secretary of state 1973–77, transformed the international situation. Nixon had a brilliant feel for foreign affairs. He knew that Americans wanted out of the Vietnam War as quickly as possible and had become weary of playing God throughout the world. The economy was in decline, hence it would be advisable to cut the defence budget. But he needed the co-operation of Moscow to get a peace settlement with Hanoi. The Soviet Union had just achieved nuclear parity with the United States: perhaps the time was propitious to negotiate an arms control agreement. Nixon was the ideal man to initiate such a policy. He had made his name as a communist-baiter and a ruthless critic of all those who had advocated a softer approach to Moscow. Kissinger, born a German Jew, was a leading specialist on nuclear weapons and foreign policy. Both men ardently desired to make their mark and neither was a team player [46–7].

They began with a weak hand. American society was tearing itself apart and not prepared to renew its leading role in the world. The deal they fashioned for Moscow came to be known as linkage: Washington would recognise the Soviet Union's strategic parity, would not attempt to interfere in the Soviet empire and would open up access to western investment and technology. In other words, the roll-back of communism had been consigned to the dustbin. The Americans wanted the Russians to help them out of Vietnam and to recognise that the superpowers had mutual interests in the Third World. The key goal was stability. The superpowers had a joint responsibility to ensure that the world did not go up in flames. For the first time since 1945, the Americans were saying to the Russians: let's do a deal. Would the Russian leadership share power with the Americans or would they decide to attempt to become number one in the world? Moscow was building up a position of strength: conventional and nuclear forces were expanding, the submarine fleet was growing, an aircraft carrier was even being built to project Soviet power throughout the world. In some areas of rocketry they were world leaders. From the point of view of the Russians, the correlation of forces was moving inexorably in their favour. Vietnam had proved to be a 'bleeding wound' for America.

The American offer of arms negotiations and what became known as détente inevitably aroused suspicion in Moscow. Washington was offering arms control negotiations just when the Russians were on the point of achieving superiority. A truce in the Third World could only signify that America wanted to hold on to what it had. However, Kosygin was aware that Russian industry needed high technology inputs and that economic growth was slowing down. Gross National Product during the years 1966–70 had grown 5 per cent annually but this was to fall to 3.1 per cent annually in 1971–75 (1988 calculations). Consumption per head of population was 5.3 per cent in 1966–70 but fell to 3.6 per cent in 1971–75. The Russian economist Khanin has argued that these data overstate performance. The second half of the 1970s saw the decline continue. GNP in 1976–80 only grew by 2.2 per cent annually and consumption growth declined to 2.6 per cent annually. These are later calculations, so the question arises about whether the leadership was aware at the time of the serious decline in economic growth. Soviet defence spending increased during the 1970s and aid to the Third World also grew, for instance to Cuba and Vietnam. There were several reports which pointed out the alarming consequences for the Soviet Union if economic reform were not considered, but Brezhnev ignored them. He was living in a fool's paradise.

CHINA CHANGES SIDES: RAPPROCHEMENT WITH AMERICA

Faced with rising tension with the Soviet Union, in November 1968 the Chinese leader Zhou Enlai proposed talks with the incoming Nixon administration. However, other, more conservative leaders ensured that the discussions did not take place. In 1969 Chinese border guards along the Ussuri river fired on their Russian counterparts, killing some on several occasions. The dispute was about which country owned islands in the river – a controversial matter since the river bed had changed course over time. Moscow considered a nuclear strike to take out China's nuclear capacity. Beijing backed off and Zhou began again to lobby for a rapprochement with Washington.

Nixon and Kissinger were greatly taken by the idea as it promised to be very fruitful. A wedge could be driven between the two communist giants and the communist movement weakened in the rest of the world. An understanding with China removed the danger of war and American troops could gradually be extricated from south-east Asia. America could concentrate its efforts on the Soviet Union and China would help to contain Moscow and Hanoi. As the Chinese were only weakly represented in the Third World, there was little danger of tension developing. Since the US public had become allergic to seeing its boys fighting and dying in other people's wars, Washington would now have to concentrate on training and arming their clients in the Third World. All these factors suggested that rapprochement with China would pay huge dividends.

President Nixon astonished the world in February 1972 when he flew to Beijing and met Mao. The main obstacle to better relations was Taiwan. The US had practised a 'two Chinas' policy: the People's Republic on the mainland and the Republic of China on Taiwan. Beijing insisted that there could only be one China and asked for US forces to leave Taiwan. Washington accepted the logic of the argument and agreed to remove its troops and installations from Taiwan, as tension subsided. If China helped the US to withdraw from

Vietnam and refrained from belligerent acts in the straits between the mainland and Taiwan, it would promote the unification of China. Moscow had not anticipated a Sino-American rapprochement and was very relieved to discover that no military alliance was contemplated. However, it was a bitter blow to discover that China, the most populous socialist state, had changed sides and was consorting with the class enemy. The rapprochement completely changed Moscow's view of the world. It would now have to think in multi-polar terms. There were three main players: Russia, America and China. A new zero sum game was emerging. If Russia pushed America too hard, it might drive it into a closer relationship with China. Thus Nixon's visit to China made Russia more amenable [29, 51, 61]. There was the awful prospect of other socialist states following China and opposing the Soviet Union. This was a condemnation of Russian foreign policy making, but, as time would tell, Moscow did not draw the correct conclusions from the Chinese débâcle.

SALT

The Nixon administration's efforts to develop an anti-ballistic missile (ABM) system worried Moscow. It was an area of technology in which the Americans were ahead and the Russians did not want to be forced to switch resources to compete. Strategic arms limitation talks (SALT) could bring benefit. There had been desultory discussions under way since 1969 but they always got bogged down in the technical detail. Nixon and Kissinger had little interest in the finer details of arms negotiations but were more concerned about the political impact of an arms deal. It would signal that the superpowers had moved from confrontation to negotiation.

The first SALT agreement was signed by Brezhnev and Nixon in Moscow in May 1972. It limited the deployment of ABM systems but little headway was made on offensive weapons systems. Agreements were signed on health and a joint space programme (the 1975 Apollo-Soyuz mission), and the two sides also agreed on certain basic principles regulating their relations, including restraint during crises and the avoidance of confrontation [18 *pp. 146–223*]. Nevertheless Nixon had pulled off a diplomatic coup: rapprochement with the nation's two main adversaries, China and Russia. The Russians were also pleased. The Americans had made concessions and formally acknowledged nuclear parity.

Brezhnev's first trip to America resulted in another summit with Nixon, in Washington, Camp David and San Clemente, California, in

June 1973. Hearings on Watergate were suspended for the meetings, during which there were agreements on agriculture, transport and cultural exchanges, and the framework for SALT II talks. Both countries promised to contact one another if nuclear war threatened to involve one or both of them. Superpower summits were becoming part of the international agenda.

THE GERMAN PROBLEM DEFUSED

In Europe, the Berlin problem was defused by the quadripartite agreement in 1971, and the East–West German agreement of 1972. For a time it appeared that West Germany might incline more to neutrality in pursuing its Ostpolitik (policy towards the east) under Willy Brandt. But when he was obliged to resign in May 1974 because an East German spy was discovered in his chancellery, his successor, Helmut Schmidt, reverted to a much closer relationship with Washington and accepted NATO modernisation. This was one instance when the brilliantly successful East German spy system in Bonn scored an own goal.

THE MIDDLE EAST

In 1967 Russian agents in Syria spread false rumours of an imminent Israeli attack and the Syrians appealed to Nasser for support. The latter demanded the removal of UN forces which were separating his troops from the Israelis, and advanced towards the Gulf of Aqaba. Israel attacked and the Six Day War was under way. Egyptian, Jordanian and Syrian troops were routed. Moscow threatened to intervene, made up for the lost equipment and sent thousands of advisers, in return for which the grateful Egyptians granted them naval rights in Egyptian ports and air bases. They were now in a position to counter the activities of the American Sixth Fleet in the Mediterranean. In 1969 Nasser began small-scale attacks against Israel, and the latter responded in 1970 with devastating air attacks far behind Egyptian lines. The Egyptian air force was no match for the Israelis and so Nasser requested, and obtained, Russian air defence systems, missiles, aircraft and pilots. The Russian pilots flew combat missions and reversed the course of the war. Moscow acceded to American calls for a cease-fire and it was announced in August 1970.

Moscow's standing as the friend of the Arabs was never higher. Nasser died a month later and the new Egyptian leader, Anwar Sadat, called on the Soviet Union to help the Arabs recapture the land lost to the Israelis. However, Moscow was more concerned with reaching an agreement with Washington. Shortly after the Brezhnev–Nixon summit in Moscow in May 1972, Sadat suddenly expelled all Russian personnel from Egypt. A high-ranking Egyptian officer commented later that one of the reasons for the decision had been the Russian claim that bases were their territory and that Egyptians could not enter them without permission. The key reason appears to have been the Egyptian realisation that America held the key to the Middle East. Russia would always place its relations with America ahead of those with the Arabs.

Egypt and Syria had been armed for war and were determined to go ahead without direct Soviet help. The attack in October 1973 took the Israelis completely by surprise, launched on Yom Kippur, when all Israelis were observing the most important religious festival. It exploded the myth of Israeli military invincibility and Moscow immediately jumped in to resupply its clients and called on other Arab states to join in. The Americans kept their distance for a week until Golda Meir, the Israeli Prime Minister, threatened to use nuclear weapons. The Americans then flew in vast amounts of supplies and the Israelis penetrated deeply into Egypt. A cease-fire, proposed by the Russians and negotiated by Kissinger, ended the fighting. But then the Israelis broke the cease-fire and Moscow threatened to send in combat troops. Nixon placed American troops on strategic alert and the superpowers were back at one another's throats.

Washington was annoyed that Moscow had known of the imminent Arab attack on Israel and had failed to warn the US. The Russian attempt to involve other Arab states in the war rankled. Brezhnev, on his part, was frustrated by the American alert which had stopped him in his tracks. The superpowers were as far apart as ever, at least in the Middle East. An increasing number of Americans were arguing that Moscow had not honoured its obligations under détente. Afterwards, Kissinger, in never-ending diplomacy, tried to patch up a Middle East settlement and conspicuously excluded the Russians [18 *pp. 404–33*; 46 *pp. 569–99*].

In May 1972, on their way back to America from signing the SALT I agreement, Nixon and Kissinger dropped in on the Shah of Iran. They concluded a secret agreement whereby Iran was to act to encourage Iraq to break its close ties with Moscow. In Vietnam, ferocious bombing of the North secured a peace agreement in January 1973, and American troops began leaving the South. In the Middle East, after Egypt had expelled Soviet military advisers in 1973, Moscow was deprived of its land and air bases, the most significant bases it had in the Third World.

The high hopes of détente faded as it became clear to the Americans that the Soviet Union was not willing to accept strategic inferiority. Kissinger was quite open about ensuring America's continued world hegemony. The SALT I agreement was to halt the race in ICBMs and submarine-launched ballistic missiles (SLBMs) when the US was way ahead in nuclear warheads. This would allow the Americans to develop rapidly systems not covered by SALT: the Trident submarine, the MX missile, the B-1 bomber and the Cruise missile [46 *pp. 256–74*]. Funding for these new weapons was a problem during the upheavals of the Vietnam War but they all went ahead, especially the Trident submarine and Cruise missile. The Nixon doctrine, declared in July 1969, aimed at arming Third World states to intervene and resist the rise of communism. This was born of the realisation that it was a bad idea to have American troops bogged down in a regional conflict far from the main Cold War areas. There was also the fact that Congress, after 1973, would not permit Nixon to dispatch troops to defend Cambodia against North Vietnam.

THE AGENDA CHANGES AS FORD TAKES OVER

Nixon's struggle for political survival in 1973–74, the death of Mao and the succession struggle which followed slowed down the intricate Nixon–Kissinger policy of rapprochement with Russia and China. Congress reasserted itself in the light of the Watergate affair and proceeded to claw back some of the power which had passed to the President. Nixon and Kissinger had conducted their foreign policy largely out of view of Congress and the people, partly because they believed that they could achieve more on their own and partly owing to their disdain for the hurly burly of democratic politics. In 1973 Congress passed an act which aimed at restraining the President's ability to deploy American military force without a declaration of war. The legislators also ordered an end to the bombing of Cambodia and passed a law which prevented US troops from being again sent to Vietnam. Relations with the Soviet Union would be tied to human rights issues, such as the freedom of Jews to emigrate from Russia. These moves restricted the ability of Nixon and Kissinger to keep the promises they had made in fashioning their intricate détente policies [*Doc. 5*].

Gerald Ford, when he took over in 1974, found himself in the same position. Brezhnev was disappointed that little American high technology flowed to the Soviet Union. Nixon needed the support of the right in his battle to survive and had to delay recognising China. The defence treaty with Taiwan remained, much to the satisfaction of the assertive enemies of 'Red' China. Gerald Ford could not improve relations with China either.

The Bretton Woods agreement of 1944 had seen the dollar become the world's leading currency. It was tied to gold and dollars would be converted into gold by the US government. The unwillingness or inability of American presidents to increase federal taxes to pay for social programmes, foreign defence and foreign aid meant that the federal budget was normally in deficit. The money markets could be tapped to cover the deficit. This system functioned extremely well for the quarter century after 1944. The US economy was the richest and most competitive in the world and American policy-makers had an unprecedented freedom of action to fashion the world in America's image. But the profligate spending by Johnson on Vietnam, the climbing budget deficits, the rise in Japanese and West German competitiveness, all contributed to the slow-down in the American economy. Johnson's overspend in Vietnam fuelled inflation and this led, in 1971, to America recording its first balance of trade deficit in the twentieth century. Foreigners now held more dollars than could be converted into gold.

Nixon bit the bullet and abandoned convertibility, devalued the dollar against the Japanese yen and the German mark (DM), and turned the economy round – at least for a short time. The Arab-Israeli war of 1973 was another demonstration of the US's declining power. A massive increase in the oil price by Iran and the Arab producers revealed how dependent America and Europe were on oil supplies from the Middle East. Saudi Arabia, the largest supplier, became the arbiter of oil prices and the Organisation of Petroleum Exporting Countries (OPEC) took over the market. There was even talk of the Arabs establishing their own banking system with the mountains of petro-dollars now piling up.

AFRICA

In Africa, the Brezhnev era got off to an unfortunate start. Its friends fell from power: first Nkrumah in Ghana in 1966, and then Keita in Mali in 1968. However, by 1979 the situation had been transformed. There was an impressive list of states which had declared Soviet socialism as their goal: Angola, Benin (Dahomey), Congo (Brazzaville), Ethiopia, Guinea, Guinea-Bissau and Mozambique. In the post-colonial aftermath, America, China and Russia competed for influence. China was in a good position in east Africa and Zambia. In the

Nigerian civil war, in the mid-1960s, the Soviets supported the federal government and China supported, diplomatically, rebel Biafra.

The revolution in Portugal in 1974 transformed the situation. Guinea-Bissau, Mozambique and Angola were to be granted their independence after years of guerrilla warfare against the colonial power. Angola brought all the competing powers together. There was also the attraction that the country was rich in minerals and oil. The MPLA, dominated by leaders of mixed race, was partly Marxist and received support from Cuba, the Soviet Union, Algeria and some western governments. The FNLA, drawing much of its strength from the Bakongo tribe, was backed by America, China, Libya and some western governments. UNITA, centred on the Ovimbundu, received aid from China and was the favourite of South Africa. In January 1975 an agreement was reached on the transfer of power from Portugal, to take place in November 1975.

Determined to prevent the emergence of a pro-Russian government, the Chinese increased arms supplies to the FNLA, followed by the Americans. The Soviets and Cubans responded in kind and helped their client, the MPLA. Fighting followed and South Africa intervened. In November Cuba sent combat troops to prevent the capital, Luanda, falling. China withdrew and Russian and Cuban involvement deepened after Congress refused Kissinger's request for more funds. This also led to the South Africans backing out. The MPLA took over as the government in early 1996, backed by Russian, Cuban (about 17,000) and some east European troops. But the Russians and Cubans supported different factions within the MPLA leadership and civil war continued for another two decades. Cuban intervention in Angola was not the first time that Castro had sent troops to black Africa. Some had arrived in Congo (Brazzaville), Guinea and Guinea-Bissau. In the Middle East, in 1973, there were about 3,000 Cuban troops.

In October 1976 Angola concluded a treaty of friendship and co-operation with the Soviet Union, and Mozambique followed in March 1977. Russia supplied the separatist movements in Eritrea and the Ogaden, while it had good relations with Somalia, where bases and port facilities were made available. When Ethiopia requested help, Russia changed sides and provided the military equipment to defeat a Somali offensive in the Ogaden. Russian and Cuban commanders turned the tide. In November 1977 Somalia expelled its Soviet advisers and told them to quit their bases. Ethiopia became a pro-Soviet socialist republic.

The communist Third World was taking shape and it appeared that Moscow had scored a decisive victory over Washington. Kissinger felt very frustrated that Congress would not provide the means to counter the communist advance on the continent. All the Americans could do was to watch from the sidelines. In Angola, the Russians could not tolerate the Americans and Chinese coming out on top and felt obliged to demonstrate to the Third World that Russia, not China, was their natural ally. The Russian military, especially the navy, were also keen to expand their presence and capabilities world-wide. They wanted bases and surveillance stations everywhere in Africa, especially on the coast. If another Middle East oil crisis erupted, they wanted to have the capability to influence the flow of oil to Europe and America.

The Russians had examined the American experience in the Third World and felt certain they could avoid the pitfalls of over-exposure. They were also buoyed up by the feeling that the correlation of forces was moving inexorably in their direction. America, engrossed with its own problems, appeared to have lost the will to challenge Russia. All these assumptions and decisions turned out to be false, with the Russians doomed to repeat the mistakes of the Americans. However, this was not the American view at the time. Détente was turning sour as all the benefits appeared to be accruing to the Russians. Brezhnev could see nothing wrong in his policy as he was merely doing what the Americans would have liked to have done.

THE HELSINKI ACCORD

The Brezhnev leadership pursued several objectives in western Europe: it wished gradually to detach the region from the United States and thereby weaken NATO; it needed the technology and know-how which increased trade would bring; it also wanted the borders of 1945 to be recognised as inviolable, thus confirming the Soviet victory in Europe in 1945. The non-aggression pact with West Germany in 1970 paved the way for the intra-German agreements of 1972 and the recognition of the GDR by the western world. These were European initiatives in which the Americans played a minor role. The first approach for a grand European conference was made in 1954. But Russia was never quite clear whether it would be better off with the Americans out of Europe or with them in Europe as a brake on the Germans.

In December 1971 the Atlantic Council accepted a proposal by the Warsaw Pact for a security conference on Europe. Preparatory talks got under way and a conference convened in Helsinki in July 1973, attended by 33 states, including NATO, the Warsaw Pact, the non-aligned movement and neutral states. Only Albania boycotted the proceedings. NATO participation meant that the US and Canada were present. The Helsinki Final Act was signed on 1 August 1975 by President Gerald Ford, Leonid Brezhnev (technically, as Party leader, he should not have signed; he only became Soviet President in 1977), and other leaders. The Russians had achieved their goal: the status quo in Europe. In order to gain their objective, the Russians had to concede, for the first time, that human rights were of a universal character and that there was to be a free exchange of ideas and people across Europe. This was basket three and Moscow had to accept it in order to get basket one: the inviolability of post-1945 frontiers. Brezhnev lived to regret this concession as it led to the founding of Helsinki monitoring groups and human rights groups in the Soviet Union. He had conceded that human rights were the legitimate concern of other states. They could now use it to criticise the Russian record on human rights. A conference on security and co-operation in Europe (CSCE) was to convene to monitor progress and promote further developments. The next meeting, in Belgrade in 1978, occurred at a time of rising east–west tension and there was precious little goodwill on show. The CSCE process was revived under Gorbachev.

A NEW PRESIDENT SOWS CONFUSION

Gerald Ford lost the presidential election in 1976 to Democrat Jimmy Carter, whose views on Russia and foreign policy were inchoate and uncertain. He rode to power on the backs of disillusioned voters who wanted a new start and a solution to all the political, economic and social problems facing America. But the President lacked experience in foreign affairs and had no knowledge of the complexities of nuclear strategy. As an able man, he would learn as he went along. He told Americans what they wanted to hear: he would do away with the old, tawdry Washington politics and base his policies on respect for human rights; he would reduce tension with the Soviet Union. But he failed to grasp that his emphasis on human rights would exacerbate tension, rather than alleviate it. On arms control, he eschewed the results of the slow, painstaking negotiations and made very radical proposals which only alarmed the Soviets.

The advice he received on foreign affairs was often contradictory as Cyrus Vance, his Secretary of State, and Zbigniew Brzezinski,

National Security Adviser, were like horses pulling in different directions [7, 67]. They both agreed on one thing – that the Soviet Union was the key country – but they differed fundamentally on how to modify Russian behaviour. Vance advocated the renaissance of détente as this would facilitate joint efforts by the superpowers to lessen tension and solve problems throughout the world. He believed that behind the ageing Brezhnev leadership stood a younger cohort, as keen as the Americans to end the confrontation between the superpowers and to concentrate on modernising their country to compete in the modern world. SALT II should be an important objective as the US needed to cut defence spending, reduce its budget deficit and, thereby, bring down inflation. The Russians could be afforded a larger role in the Middle East with something approaching an American-Russian condominium. This would ensure that Moscow would not succumb to the temptation of promoting extremist Arab regimes. In Africa, the Russians would soon learn what the Americans had learned in Vietnam: expending energy and resources there would lead to disillusionment. Africa was, after all, of marginal significance to the superpowers. China was not as significant as Nixon and Kissinger had believed. The danger for America was that China could cause tension which would harm the development of détente with Russia. Vance's goal, therefore, was to get the Russians to see the world through his spectacles.

Brzezinski was quite a different person. As a native Pole, he had great respect for Russians but did not trust them. Moscow would not modify its behaviour out of the goodness of its heart. It would have to be obliged to do so. To this end, America should go for strategic superiority, strengthen NATO, attract the Chinese to its side against Russia, undermine Russia's hold on eastern Europe and outface the Soviets world-wide. If SALT II were signed it would be a bonus. Brzezinski adopted the typical Polish view that the best way to deal with the Russians was to beat them. Hence Carter got conflicting advice and, as an amateur, tried to evolve policy which reflected both viewpoints. This made him a laughing stock to many.

Vance's approach was not viable in the late 1970s. Brezhnev, now partly dependent on drugs, was becoming incoherent at top meetings and had ignored all the warnings about the need for economic reform. Those around him preferred that he stay in office as it allowed them to build up their own empires. Those who had aspirations to succeed him wanted him to stay until the propitious moment for their succession bid arrived. The gerontocrats put personal interest ahead of national interest. Nevertheless, the tide of world affairs appeared to be flowing in Moscow's direction. Communists took power in Afghanistan in April 1978, on their own initiative. The Shah of Iran had to flee his country in January 1979, and this undermined the American position in the Middle East. Ayatollah Khomeni turned out to be virulently anti-American and anti-western. In the Caribbean, Grenada became pro-communist, and in Central America Guatemala sided with Moscow. It all appeared as if the Soviet Union's position in the world were strengthening and that the future would be even brighter.

Carter did register many foreign policy successes but they were almost all achieved at the expense of the Soviet Union. Anwar Sadat, of Egypt, concluding that the Soviets could not broker a Middle East peace, accepted American mediation in the conflict with Israel. This produced the Camp David Accords and Sadat astonished the world in 1977 by going to Israel to demonstrate that peace was possible between the two countries. Pushed by Carter, the Israelis agreed to return the Sinai peninsula to Egypt, who in return would recognise – the first Arab state to do so – the state of Israel. The latter had now the right to exist. This démarche annoyed the Russians as they had been expressly excluded from the peace process. Predictably, Moscow did not recognise the agreement and sided with Arab states which continued to deny Israel the right to exist. Superpower tension in the Middle East was as great as before [35, 50, 56, 60].

The United States finally normalised its relations with the People's Republic of China in December 1978. Carter was always torn between soothing the Soviets, Vance's preference, and demonstrating American muscle to them, Brzezinski's advice. The former had little interest in China and did not think that improving relations with Beijing at the expense of relations with Moscow was sensible. Deng Xiaoping, who emerged as China's main leader in 1978, was keen to use the Vance–Brzezinski dissonance to benefit China. Beijing was apprehensive about Soviet-American détente and wanted to give Vietnam a bloody nose, without the threat of Russian intervention.

Deng became the first Chinese leader to visit the United States, in January 1979, and the visit was a great success. He asked to visit the space centre at Houston, where he climbed into a simulator and was fascinated by the technology which brought a spacecraft down to earth. Washington turned a blind eye when Chinese forces penetrated North Vietnam. Despite criticising the course of Sino-American relations, the Russians were keen to slow down the arms race [65].

CARTER AND BREZHNEV REACH AGREEMENT ON SALT II BUT ON LITTLE ELSE

After seven years of endeavour, SALT II was signed by Jimmy Carter and Leonid Brezhnev in Vienna in June 1979. A draft SALT II agreement had been floated at the Vladivostok summit between Gerald Ford and Leonid Brezhnev in November 1974, but progress had been slow thereafter due to claims that too much was being conceded to the Soviet Union under détente. The Russian invasion of Afghanistan, in December 1979, led to President Carter withdrawing the treaty for ratification in the Senate, in January 1980. However, both sides pledged to observe the treaty limits voluntarily. The next stage in arms talks, which opened in Geneva in June 1982, assumed the name of strategic arms reduction talks, or START. This was a psychological leap forward, with the superpowers now talking about reducing their arsenals.

Carter and Brezhnev fell out over a Soviet combat brigade in Cuba. It and other troops had been there since the Cuban missile crisis and this was permitted, according to the deal done to end the crisis. Pressed by the right, Carter demanded the brigade be withdrawn and Brezhnev refused. This unnecessary conflict rumbled on during the summer and autumn of 1979. However, it was soon overshadowed by a much more serious event.

In November 1979 Ayatollah Khomeni's followers seized the US embassy, holding those inside hostage (the siege lasted 14 months). This humiliated the United States and, inevitably, President Carter became another man under siege. Why could he not use American power to free the hostages in Iran? In December 1979 Carter's Soviet policy collapsed [62].

5   COLD WAR II: 1979–1985

DÉTENTE FAILS TO SATISFY AMERICAN ASPIRATIONS

By the mid-1970s it was clear that Kissinger's policy of détente had failed [*Doc. 5*]. It had rested on the assumption that a linkage could be established. Washington's improved relations with Moscow would depend on Moscow's willingness not to challenge Washington in the Third World. SALT I and increasing Russian-American trade should satisfy Moscow. It did not. Brezhnev could not resist helping America's enemies to press home their advantage. In Vietnam, the communist victory in 1975 owed much to the arms supplied by the Soviet Union. In Africa, Cuba and the Soviet Union embarrassed the United States. The volatility of Third World politics began to reveal that the two superpowers were no longer masters there. The US and the Soviet Union simply did not possess the economic power to ensure that their will was done. Furthermore, Western Europe and Japan were developing rapidly and demanding a greater say in international economic policy.

In Europe, the collapse of the right-wing dictatorship in Portugal in 1974, the fall of the military dictatorship in Greece, also in 1974, and the death of Franco, the Spanish dictator, in 1975, alarmed Kissinger. Communist parties were influential in all three states and it also appeared possible that the communists in France and Italy, the Eurocommunists, would enter into coalition governments. This had alarming implications for NATO as all these states, except Spain, were members. As it turned out, Kissinger's gloom was unfounded. All three states took the democratic path and Spain joined NATO.

In 1976 Kissinger declared that he would no longer use the term détente. What was to succeed it – something between it and Cold War II, or Cold War II? During the 1976 election campaign, Jimmy Carter reflected the anti-military mood of the voters by criticising the one-sided emphasis on military power to achieve security. However, he also took umbrage at the weakness of Gerald Ford at Helsinki and the ground he had given to the Soviets in the SALT II memorandum, agreed at the Vladivostok summit. Either he was confused or he was pitching for votes from the right and left.

CARTER'S MIXED RECORD

In office, Carter pursued even deeper cuts in a SALT II agreement, although he did not succeed in getting these into the agreement signed in 1979. He did not engage in the anti-Russian rhetoric which was the common currency of many previous presidents. The weakness of the US economy demanded he pay greater attention to reflation, in collaboration with the developed market economies. Human rights became important, as did north–south issues. The US would no longer support repressive regimes simply because they were anti-communist. Government was to be more open, to heal the wounds of the Nixon–Kissinger years.

On the other hand, Carter cancelled the B-1 bomber in 1977, and the development of Cruise missiles. The main reason was expense but the switch allowed the development of a new Stealth bomber. Defence expenditure climbed under Carter. During negotiations on a SALT II treaty, Helmut Schmidt, the West German chancellor, and the Russians, wanted European theatre weapons (medium-range nuclear weapons) to be included. Carter, following Brzezinski's advice, declined. Cyrus Vance informed Moscow in March 1977 that these weapons would not be included in discussions [65].

When Schmidt finally gave way to Carter, the Soviet response was to deploy SS20s in eastern Europe in late 1977. This was a tactical mistake by Moscow and handed the initiative to NATO, always having to find ways of balancing Soviet conventional superiority. In January 1979 the west decided to deploy Cruise and Pershing II missiles. Carter went on the offensive against the Soviet Union in 1977 by declaring that it could be undermined in six states: China, Vietnam, Somalia, Iraq, Algeria and Cuba. This was in sharp contrast to Kissinger's policy which now appeared defensive.

Besides rising defence expenditure, there was the added bonus that weapons were becoming more accurate. In July 1980 Carter signed a presidential decree that placed emphasis on targeting military objectives, rather than economic targets and the population, as before. This made possible a limited war, one aimed only at certain military targets. Here the Americans had an advantage. Only about one-quarter of their ICBMs were on land, whereas the Soviets had about three-quarters on their terrain. Conventional forces were not forgotten. The President signed decrees establishing a rapid reaction force which could intervene in the Third World when the occasion arose. Carter had promised to withdraw US forces from South Korea but, in office, quickly reversed this decision. He also turned a blind eye to human rights' violations there. Another campaign promise – to scale down quickly arms deliveries to the Third World – was forgotten, and El Salvador, just to name one instance, was armed to counter the Sandinistas in Nicaragua [28].

Carter had downgraded the significance of China to the US, but in August 1979 Vice-President Mondane went to Beijing to sign a secret agreement permitting the Americans to install an electronic listening station in Xinjiang, in western China, near the Soviet border. China, in another agreement, reached in Beijing in January 1980, was to receive US military equipment for the first time. This alarmed the Russians and may have convinced them to sign a SALT II agreement, even though it did not include European theatre nuclear weapons.

DISASTROUS DECISION-MAKING IN MOSCOW:
INTERVENTION IN AFGHANISTAN

Moscow intervened in Afghanistan [Doc. 9] believing the mild-mannered American President would hardly raise an eyebrow. A KGB report informed Brezhnev that the country could be taken over in a few weeks, then a few months, then six months, and so on. The Vietnam syndrome was this time returning to haunt the Soviet Union. Carter took Brzezinski's advice. He went over the top, described the invasion as the most serious danger to peace since 1945, halted a grain export contract with Moscow and told US athletes not to participate in the 1980 Olympic games in Moscow. Other nations should follow suit. This mortified Moscow and it responded by not sending athletes to the 1984 Los Angeles games. Only Romania broke the eastern boycott. The Carter doctrine was proclaimed, also in 1980, according to which the Persian Gulf was of vital strategic importance to America. America would deal directly with any outside force seeking to gain control of the Persian Gulf region. The Russians were not to go anywhere near it.

Russia's intervention in Afghanistan was taken by a handful of top leaders but they ignored Soviet military reservations about the wisdom of getting involved in domestic Afghan politics. Brezhnev's main worry appears to have been that a new leader might be under the influence of China or America. This might threaten the Soviet position in Central Asia. If Moscow failed to come to the aid of its friends in

Afghanistan this might lead other communist leaders around the world to conclude that Moscow no longer had the willpower to counter the American threat. But the Brezhnev leadership failed completely to appreciate the negative impact the invasion would have on the Islamic world, first and foremost in the Middle East [*Doc. 11*]. At a time when America's authority was very low, Moscow was throwing Washington a lifeline by uniting the Middle East against Russia.

By 1979, only China could express any satisfaction at the evolution of events during the 1970s. The Americans and Russians were profoundly disillusioned: strategic parity had brought few dividends for the Soviet Union and détente had become a term of abuse in many American mouths. Moscow's drive for supremacy had crumbled and had provoked accelerated defence spending. The war in Afghanistan contributed to the election of Ronald Reagan as President. The champion of the right was unequivocal about the Soviet Union – it was the 'evil empire'. Russians felt deeply insulted by this term [9 *pp. 188– 218*; 18 *pp. 623–85*].

CARTER, BRZEZINSKI AND COLD WAR II

It was Brzezinski who articulated the thinking behind Cold War II, which can be dated from Soviet intervention in Afghanistan. He was keen to involve the Soviet Union in a military and economic race which would increase political and social strains within that country. He was not against nuclear war *per se*, believing that the Soviet Union would come off worse. The abandonment of détente was blamed, of course, on Moscow. Its lack of restraint in Afghanistan proved the pretext to announce the beginning of the new cold war. It marked the end of the policy of deterrence which America had pursued since the 1960s [7].

It is ironic that Carter continued to be perceived as a weak President. He had suffered the humiliation of the Iranian hostage crisis, the continued presence of the Soviet combat brigade in Cuba, and the Russian slap in the face in invading Afghanistan. But there was another side to his presidency. He increased the military budget, created a rapid reaction force, deployed the MX missile and concluded secret military deals with the Chinese. Domestically, his greatest failure was his inability to turn the economy round. Hence he was seen by voters as a failure, domestically and internationally. He prepared the way for Ronald Reagan who only had to promise to re-establish America's hegemony in the world and to stimulate economic growth for many voters to choose him. There was no evidence that he, uninterested in foreign and security affairs and economics, would be any more successful than Carter, but, as an actor, he was brilliant at creating an aura of optimism. Surely such an imposing, articulate man had to succeed.

A NEW PRESIDENT AND A NEW DEPARTURE

President Ronald Reagan adopted a simple black and white view of the Russians. Drugged by a utopian ideology into believing they were destined to take over the world, they were addicted to lying and cheating at every opportunity. Morality to them was relative. If a policy advanced the interests of the Soviet Union and communism world-wide, it was moral. Failure, of course, was immoral. There was no point in negotiating agreements with the Russians since they were bound to break them. The way to deal with Moscow was to build up American nuclear superiority and combat Soviet interventions in the Third World.

Reagan presided over an extraordinary expansion of the military-industrial complex in the United States. Although 1981 was a poor year economically, defence expenditure in 1982 was to increase 13 per cent, and over 8 per cent in succeeding years. The CIA budget went up even faster. The American military began to think it could initiate and win a nuclear war. One option was to prepare for a six-month nuclear war with Russia. The new weapons were more accurate and could take out Soviet military and political targets with surgical strikes. Communications were being developed to function in America after a Soviet nuclear strike. The Reagan administration claimed to have discovered a window of vulnerability through which a Soviet first strike would devastate America, and this highly dubious claim was used to justify the extraordinary expansion of the US arsenal in the early 1980s. In Europe, the use of the neutron bomb and chemical weapons might even be considered. The administration returned to the concept of linkage. In 1981 the United States informed the Soviet Union that the latter's response to US proposals on Afghanistan and Cambodia would be the litmus test for their relations. Washington wanted a Russian retreat there.

Despite his military's thoughts of starting and winning a nuclear war against the Soviet Union, President Reagan had a horror of such weapons. His major objective was to ensure that no Russian first strike was ever launched against America. Later he was to concur with Gorbachev's goal of eliminating nuclear weapons, all nuclear weapons.

The Russians were alarmed about the deployment of Pershing II and Cruise missiles, whose accuracy and speed made them extremely difficult to counter. They believed they had found a secret weapon in their battle to ensure these missiles were never deployed – the western peace movement. Anti-nuclear feeling was running very high in western Europe in the early 1980s, and consequently the west European states which were to receive the missiles only wanted them as a last resort. They would have preferred the United States to reach an agreement with the Soviet Union which would make their deployment unnecessary. If the Soviets would remove their SS4s, SS5s and SS20s, there would be no need for Pershing II and Cruise missiles in Europe. This was a good tactic since it takes two to reach an agreement.

In Geneva the Americans began discussing an intermediate-range nuclear force (INF) agreement. Congress instructed the President to resume the SALT talks, renamed the strategic arms reduction talks (START). For the first time, the arsenals of the superpowers might be reduced. Given the attitude of the Reagan administration to the Soviet Union, these negotiations promised to be long drawn out.

There was another issue on which America's European allies did not see eye to eye with the US. When martial law was proclaimed in Poland in 1981 [*Doc. 10*], the US announced economic sanctions against Poland and the Soviet Union and asked the Europeans to follow suit. One sensitive item was the natural gas pipeline to carry Soviet gas to western Europe. Washington requested that western Europe cease supplying pipes and equipment, but such was the negative European reaction that the Americans backed off and the pipeline went ahead [*27 pp. 203–33*].

Against all the odds, the chief American and Soviet negotiators, while walking in the woods near Geneva, arrived at a compromise on intermediate range weapons. But the White House was not pleased as it wanted talks but no agreement. In the end, Washington was spared acute embarrassment by Moscow turning down the deal as well. The Brezhnev leadership had deluded themselves into believing that Reagan was a President with whom they could do business. They greatly disliked Carter because of his zig-zag policies, his inability to meet commitments and his violent rhetoric after their intervention in Afghanistan. As the US economy was in bad shape, it was logical that Reagan would welcome a deal to trim his defence budget. But he was a bitter disappointment to the ailing Brezhnev. The latter was unaware that it was the Soviet Union which urgently needed to cut its defence spending, rather than the US.

ANDROPOV AND REAGAN: MISSED OPPORTUNITIES

Brezhnev died in November 1982 and was succeeded by Yury Andropov. His first priority was to increase the effectiveness of the Soviet economy by improving labour discipline. He knew that growth had slowed down (in reality, it had stopped) but was unaware that the Soviet Union was facing a systemic crisis. It was soon discovered that he was terminally ill, dying of kidney failure, however, and so he was unable to make much impact on the Soviet Union. He was a well informed Russian leader as the country had built up a competent group of specialists on foreign policy. The military dominated security policy. The specialists were aware that the expansion of the Soviet nuclear arsenal and the penetration of the Third World had contributed to America's more belligerent stance [Doc. 11]. Moscow, like Washington, was attempting to gain superiority. As long as this continued, a slowing down of the arms race was unlikely. The Soviet Union would have to offer the United States something tangible to entice the latter to change its attitude to Russia.

In the early 1980s Moscow perceived, for the first time, that the burden of empire was becoming too heavy. Subsidies were required for more and more countries: Cuba, Vietnam, Afghanistan, Ethiopia, to name only the most onerous. The billions of dollars needed to support these regimes were needed to reinvigorate the domestic economy. The war in Afghanistan was unpopular at home and eroding the status of the Soviet military. It was also promoting drug addiction and trafficking and corruption in the military.

Andropov placed too much reliance on the western peace movements to halt the deployment of Pershing II and Cruise missiles. Arms negotiations in Geneva became formal as the US tabled proposals which it knew Moscow would not accept. Andropov's illness also contributed to a lack of flexibility in Soviet policy. On one occasion, when the American negotiators requested Moscow's latest position on arms, a Soviet delegate opened his briefcase and pulled out a copy of that day's Pravda. He then pushed it across the table. Needless to say, the US delegation had already been briefed on that day's Pravda. In November the Soviet delegation simply walked out of the INF negotiations, blaming the Americans for their breakdown.

In March 1983 President Reagan suddenly announced a startling initiative, the Strategic Defence Initiative, or Star Wars programme. He had been fascinated for a long time about the concept of protecting the United States from missile attack by erecting a shield in space. It was consistent with his horror of nuclear war. Had this been feasible, it would have been the dream weapon. Despite being called defensive, it could provide the shield behind which the US military could launch a nuclear first strike. Few US scientists took it seriously, and even fewer Russian scientists, but the Soviet military could not ignore it. The Soviet military did not wish to devote resources to it, but if the Americans went ahead they would have to. The major objection, however, remained unarticulated in public. The Russians were alarmed about the research and development implications of the SDI project: it might lead to a technological breakthrough in a related defence field. US negotiators now had a bargaining chip in dealing with the Soviets. Moscow launched violent propagandistic attacks on SDI, thereby convincing many observers that the Americans had something the Russians feared. It was illogical to claim simultaneously that SDI was science fiction and then claim it was a threat to world peace. SDI was thus at the centre of arms talks during the whole Reagan administration.

The low point during the Andropov–Reagan era was the shooting down in September 1983, by Soviet fighters, of the Korean airliner, KA007, en route from Alaska to Seoul, killing all 269 passengers and crew, including some American citizens. It had strayed into Soviet airspace and was taken for a spy plane. The Russians first of all denied shooting it down and then insisted that it was a spy plane. Reagan mirrored American and international outrage and Russia was belaboured in the United Nations. Andrei Gromyko, lost for words, simply turned his back on some film evidence shown by the Americans. The situation was compounded by the choice of Marshal Nikolai Ogarkov, the highly capable Chief of the General Staff, as the Russian spokesman. A poor diplomat, he made no attempt to express regret or apologise for the incident, merely stating that it would be repeated if another spy plane penetrated Soviet air space. His performance was technically brilliant but sent shivers down western spines. The Soviet decision-making process was clearly in need of reform. Part of the problem had been that the Commander-in-Chief of the armed forces, Yury Andropov, was terminally ill. In Geneva in December 1983, talks on reducing conventional forces ended without agreement on further meetings.

FAILURE AND SUCCESS FOR AMERICA

A disastrous episode for American policy in the Middle East was their involvement in the Lebanese civil war. After Israel had invaded Lebanon and ignited a civil war, the US intervened in an attempt to restore order. In October 1983 a terrorist drove a lorry packed with explosives up to the Marine compound and killed 241 Americans. Reagan then ordered those marines who had survived to ships off the coast. Moscow avoided direct involvement, unsure about US and Israeli reaction, and restricted itself to arming the Syrians who gained the upper hand in the Lebanese civil war. A mortal enemy of America and Israel, Iran, was also involved.

Things went better for the US in Grenada, a small island in the Caribbean, the same month. A powerful American force overwhelmed the Cubans and North Koreans advising and protecting the communists who had seized power. Cuba's Castro fumed about US imperialism but Moscow did nothing – it was too risky to intervene in America's backyard. It continued to provide some arms to the Sandinistas but eschewed direct intervention [Doc. 6]. The US had re-established hegemony in the Americas.

THE GROUND IS PREPARED FOR BETTER RELATIONS WITH RUSSIA

The appointment of George Shultz, in June 1982, as Secretary of State heralded a more pragmatic approach to Russia. The United States was becoming more self-confident and things were not going economically very well in the Soviet Union. Reagan, despite his reference to the Soviet Union as the 'evil empire' and calls for a crusade of freedom, was keen to visit the country, and also China. Shultz explained that an improvement in relations was necessary before a visit could take place.

Reagan had a secret meeting with Anatoly Dobrynin, the Soviet ambassador, in February 1983. He talked about constructive dialogue and reducing tension between the superpowers, but nothing happened because the Moscow establishment was, understandably, very suspicious of Reagan, and Andropov was terminally ill. In January 1984 Reagan made an uncharacteristically hopeful speech about improving relations and George Shultz impressed on Andrei Gromyko, the Russian Foreign Minister, that Reagan meant what he said. Andropov sent a secret letter to the President informing him of his interest in promoting contact between them. Again nothing came of this as Andropov died and was succeeded by the ill Chernenko. The best way to improve superpower relations was for the leaders to meet face to face. The likelihood of this, however, was slim, given the fact that Chernenko was more concerned about breathing (he suffered from emphysema) than meeting the President [63].

In September 1984 Reagan met Andrei Gromyko for the first time, while the latter was attending the UN. When Reagan was re-elected President in November 1984, he and Shultz set out to improve relations with Moscow. In November it was announced that Gromyko and Shultz would meet in January 1985 to discuss arms control. In Geneva, Gromyko and Shultz agreed on three sets of talks: START, INF, and defensive systems, including those based in space. Then Chernenko died in March 1985 and his successor was Mikhail Sergeevich Gorbachev, the youngest member of the Russian leadership. He was destined to improve relations with the United States to an extent undreamed of by Reagan or Shultz. Cold War II was over [9 *pp. 219–30; 18 pp. 1125–46; 34; 47 pp. 286–320; 58 pp. 18–75*].

REAGAN IMPROVES RELATIONS WITH CHINA

In April 1984 Reagan was granted his wish to visit China. Shultz managed to wean him away from seeing Taiwan as China and towards appreciating the importance of the People's Republic for the United States. Reagan's intelligence was not that of an academic but that of an actor, and this placed a premium on those who wrote the script. The President found economics, strategic theory, and all disciplines which required a long concentration span, boring. He had a sense of what the ordinary person wanted to hear and he was extremely skilled in delivering a message. Only he could present a change in policy towards Russia as something absolutely natural. Those advisers who proved most adept at gaining his ear, promised to be very influential. Shultz turned out to be one of them. As the champion of the right, Reagan had always been surrounded by those who were close to Chiang Kai-shek and Taiwan and who dreamed of one day returning to power in Beijing. As a pragmatist, Shultz knew this was nonsense, perhaps dangerous nonsense. There were advantages to Washington in good relations with Beijing, but the closeness of the later Carter years was gone and the 'China card', playing Beijing off against Moscow, existed more in theory than reality [29].

6 NEW POLITICAL THINKING AND THE END OF THE COLD WAR: 1985–1991

Gorbachev's first priority was to accelerate Soviet economic growth. He was aware that the existing order was inefficient. There were over 100 situation papers on the economy on his desk when he took over, the product of an endeavour initiated by Andropov. The major goals of reform were to strengthen the Communist Party and the country. He was aware that the military burden was too onerous (it proved impossible to quantify it accurately) and warned that if reform did not succeed the Soviet Union might lose its superpower status by 2000. The Russians thought the Americans were unlikely to sustain their rises in defence spending due to the huge rise in the budget deficits. Gorbachev thought that reforming the existing Soviet system would suffice and only realised in 1989 that the country was in systemic crisis. In order to save money on defence, he needed a meeting with Reagan to wean him away from SDI and to initiate arms negotiations which would halt and, eventually, reverse the arms race. Since the superpowers could destroy one another many times over, there was no point in making more nuclear weapons.

THE NEW POLITICAL THINKING

An early move was to remove Andrei Gromyko, known as 'Grim Grom', as Foreign Minister, and replace him with Eduard Shevardnadze, a charming, volatile Georgian. The Gorbachev–Shevardnadze duo revolutionised foreign policy and won hearts and minds worldwide. They operated according to what became known as the new political thinking [Doc. 12]. The main components of this were:

- confrontation between the superpowers is counter-productive since any tangible gain by one side stimulates the other to match and improve on it;

- military power does not guarantee security; it can only be achieved by political means and the search for common solutions;

- the security of one state is not enhanced if it is achieved at the expense of another state;

- the conflict between the superpowers in the Third World had brought Moscow little tangible gain, indeed it had exacerbated tension between them; Russia and America should combine their efforts to solve Third World problems together;

- all states were interdependent, hence their security depended on interaction with others;

- common universal values, such as human rights, the non-use of force in order to solve political problems, democracy and freedom of conscience, should inform foreign policy making;

- the class approach to foreign policy formation should therefore be dropped in favour of the common interests of humankind;

- the Soviet Union was a normal state which was not seeking world hegemony; it wished to work closely with all other states.

Afghanistan was a major stumbling block in this new policy as it antagonised the west and the Islamic world. The communist Third World was becoming a greater burden as not a single state appeared capable of sustainable economic growth. One estimate put the annual cost of subventioning Cuba, Vietnam, Ethiopia, Afghanistan and the others, at US$40 billion. Furthermore, all east European states were heavily in debt to the Soviet Union.

The Reagan administration continued to combat the friends of the Soviet Union world-wide. In Nicaragua more aid was extended to the Contras, trained by the CIA. The Mujahidin were backed in Afghanistan, and those opposed to the Soviet-friendly regimes in Angola, Cambodia, Mozambique and elsewhere were encouraged.

THE GORBACHEV–REAGAN SUMMITS

When Vice-President George Bush attended Chernenko's funeral he handed Gorbachev a letter from the President proposing a meeting in America. Two weeks later, Gorbachev agreed in principle, but suggested they meet in Moscow. In June, they agreed their first meeting would take place in Geneva in November 1985. During the spring and summer of 1985 Gorbachev and Reagan exchanged letters quite frequently and this permitted both sides to float proposals to discover if there was any common ground.

In October Gorbachev introduced the concept of 'reasonable sufficiency' in assessing the size of armed forces. The Soviet side devoted considerable energy to developing a position on arms control, with the Politburo drawing up a negotiating position, in consultation with the foreign and defence ministries, the international department of the Party Central Committee, and the KGB. On substantive points there were guidelines on how far Gorbachev was to go. A fall-back position was also worked out. On the most contentious issues – on conventional and nuclear arms cuts – the foreign ministry acted as the co-ordinator. It was later superseded by a special Politburo commission, chaired by Lev Zaikov, which received submissions from ministries, the KGB, academic institutes and leading specialists. Zaikov or Shevardnadze would then brief Gorbachev, who would introduce his own ideas and a final version would be submitted to the Politburo. Hence the day-to-day evolution of Soviet foreign policy rested with Shevardnadze. It is difficult to say if proposals originated with him or Gorbachev. The Soviet leader was mainly concerned with domestic affairs but foreign affairs assumed great significance towards the end of his period in office.

The Geneva summit was a watershed in relations. Gorbachev's attitude to Reagan was that he was more than a conservative, he was a political dinosaur. The American President reciprocated by viewing the Soviet Union as Upper Volta with missiles, but potentially a threat to the free world. He despised everything about communism. Reagan's dislike of Russia and Russians was abstract – he had never visited the country. However, the few Russians he had met, such as Dobrynin and Gromyko, he liked. Geneva was regarded as a success by both sides. The personal chemistry worked. One of the reasons for this was that Gorbachev noticed that Reagan did not like detail. So the two leaders talked in general terms and got on well. Reagan was keen to get across the message that a nuclear war could not be won, so should not be fought. The Russians proposed that the two superpowers should issue a statement that neither would be the first to launch a nuclear war. The US objected to this as it precluded an American nuclear response to a Soviet conventional invasion of western Europe. The compromise reached was to agree to prevent any war between them, whether nuclear or conventional. They also pledged not to seek military superiority. On Afghanistan, Gorbachev made it clear that the Soviets did not intend to stay there and were seeking a political settlement.

In January 1986 the goal of a nuclear free world was spelled out at a conference in Moscow at the Ministry of Foreign Affairs. In May 1986 the new political thinking in foreign policy was formally launched. Gennady Gerasimov, renowned for his suave performances and one-liners, such as the Sinatra doctrine 'we'll do it our way', became the foreign ministry press spokesman. The ministry had been found wanting during the Chernobyl nuclear disaster in April 1986, when it had claimed that there had been no disaster, and subsequently new-style diplomats, long on persuasion and short on ideological cant, began to take over.

Reagan's commitment to SDI, reiterated at Geneva, did not deter the Russians. In the months following the summit they launched proposal after proposal to end the arms race. Everything now appeared to be negotiable and Moscow's flexibility caught Washington off guard. In January 1986 Gorbachev dramatically proposed the phasing out of nuclear weapons by 2000. On intermediate-range missiles, the Soviet position was now almost that of the Americans. Moscow was willing to accept limits on ICBMs and the balance of conventional forces in Europe. Soviet troops, perceived as threatening by NATO, could be redeployed. The Russian military were quite happy to go along with cuts in strategic arms, if they did not make the Soviet Union vulnerable. However, they drew the line at conventional reductions and here Gorbachev had a fight on his hands. In February 1986 Gorbachev referred to Afghanistan as a 'running sore' and signalled that Russia wanted out in order to improve relations with Washington.

The American response, in April 1986, was to strike at Libya, with the intent of killing Qaddafi, the Libyan leader judged an accomplice in a bomb attack which had killed US servicemen. The CIA began to supply the Mujahidin with Stinger missiles which were promptly used to bring down Soviet helicopters. In May Reagan declared that the US would no longer observe the unratified SALT II agreement.

The first direct conflict between the two leaders occurred in August 1986, when the Americans arrested Gennady Zakharov, a Soviet UN employee, when he was on the point of purchasing classified documents. The KGB responded by arresting Nicholas Daniloff, the Moscow correspondent of *US News and World Report*. Reagan wrote a personal letter to Gorbachev confirming that Daniloff was not a spy, but George Shultz and the editor of *US News and World Report* were aware that Daniloff had acquired secret Soviet documents and photographs and had passed them on to the State Department. Shultz was furious when he discovered that the CIA had used Daniloff as a contact with a Soviet source and had discussed him on an open telephone line; he regarded the whole episode as a CIA ploy to oppose his efforts to improve relations with the Soviet Union.

During the three weeks Gorbachev took to respond to Reagan's letter, the US ordered 25 Soviet UN employees, whom they deemed to be engaged in intelligence gathering, out of the country. Moscow was warned that if it retaliated more would go. The Americans also demanded that Yury Orlov, a prominent human rights campaigner, be released and permitted to move to the US, along with his wife. (They eventually left.) Shultz's excellent personal relations with Shevardnadze, which included taking the Foreign Minister on a boating trip down the Potomac and serenading him with 'Georgia on my mind', made it possible to find a solution. Daniloff was released, Zakharov was expelled and Reagan then announced the Reykjavik summit, in October 1986. However, this was not the end of the affair. After the summit Moscow ordered out five US diplomats and Washington retaliated by sending 55 Soviet diplomats packing. Why did Gorbachev take KGB advice and order out the American diplomats? It may have been in pique after failing at the summit to get what he wanted from Reagan [54].

US Congress restricted financial support for anti-communist movements throughout the world. The Reagan administration countered by seeking donations from rich supporters and foreign rulers, such as the Saudis. To secure the release of American hostages held by pro-Iranian terrorists in Lebanon, it was decided to sell arms secretly to the Iranians and to use the proceeds to arm the Nicaraguan Contras. This began to embarrass Reagan when the story broke in late 1986.

In the run-up to the Reykjavik summit, Gorbachev offered more and more concessions. ICBMs could be eliminated over ten years. US and Soviet tactical nuclear weapons could be removed from Europe. The sticking point, as before, was SDI. Initially, Gorbachev gained the upper hand. Noting that Reagan's answers were vague, the Russian leader then posed specific questions. The President then shuffled his cards to find the right answer but some of them fell on the floor. When he had gathered them up they were out of order. Reagan accepted Gorbachev's goal of the elimination of nuclear weapons but refused to agree that testing of SDI should be restricted to the laboratory. The President could have agreed to laboratory testing without slowing down the project, but he was unaware of this.

The two leaders came tantalisingly close to an official agreement but unofficially they had agreed on more issues than ever before. The Soviets now accepted on-site inspection and human rights as a subject for negotiation. When he returned to Moscow, Gorbachev gave vent to his frustration at a Politburo meeting, using insulting, demeaning language to describe Reagan. However, when he had calmed down, he confessed that the two leaders were 'doomed to co-operate'. Formal failure at Reykjavik resulted in a better INF agreement in 1987, when all missiles were eliminated. Britain and France would have resisted giving up their nuclear deterrents if Reagan's acceptance of the elimination of all nuclear weapons had remained [*Docs 13 and 14*].

Reagan pursued four objectives in his relations with Gorbachev: arms reduction, withdrawing from military confrontation in third countries, building respect for human rights, and raising the iron curtain. Gradually the Soviet side came to realise that progress on these issues could be of mutual benefit. If progress were made on one issue it would not be that the Soviets had lost out to the Americans. Zero sum diplomacy was coming to an end. The breakthrough came in November 1987, when Shultz and Shevardnadze reached agreement on verification.

In December Gorbachev travelled to Washington and he and Reagan signed the epoch-making INF agreement. It eliminated a whole class of nuclear weapons: those carried by intermediate-range ballistic missiles, over 2,500 in all. It was the first arms agreement signed by the superpowers since 1979. The verification procedures were so intrusive that American officials began to worry that the Soviets might learn too much about US defence. On the last day of his visit, on 10 December, on his way to the White House, Gorbachev suddenly instructed his driver to stop. He got out and started working the crowd. He was enthusiastically received and was exhilarated by the warmth and emotion he encountered. Over lunch, he informed everyone that his reception had made a deep impression on him.

Psychologically, this came at a vital moment for him. At home, he was finding it harder and harder to counter the populist appeal of Boris Yeltsin and opposition to perestroika in the Party and the country. As things became more complex domestically, they flowered internationally. Gorbymania can be said to have been born in Washington in December 1987. He was adored and he loved it. In future, when he felt battered at home, all he had to do to recover his aplomb was to go abroad and be feted. Doubters abroad were being silenced while domestically they were becoming more strident and numerous. The Washington summit cemented a partnership with the US and the end of the Cold War was in sight. Things began to change also in Russia. A softer line on human rights was taken and Jews who wished to emigrate were released from detention and permitted to leave. The Russian Orthodox Church, with the support of the regime, marked the millennium of Christianity in Russia, churches were refurbished and reconsecrated.

In February 1988 Gorbachev announced that Soviet forces would be withdrawn from Afghanistan, and an agreement on this was signed in April. In May Russian troops began to leave Mongolia and it was hinted that they could soon begin quitting eastern Europe. Reagan travelled to Moscow for his last summit with Gorbachev and on 1 June they exchanged the instruments of ratification which implemented the INF treaty. Reagan strolled in Red Square with Gorbachev, and when asked by journalists if he still regarded the Soviet Union as an evil empire, answered in the negative. He had changed his mind, as had many Americans. Only 30 per cent now saw Russia as evil and threatening.

In December 1988 at the UN, Gorbachev announced that the Soviet Union would reduce unilaterally its forces by half a million within two years. Soviet troops stationed in the GDR, Czechoslovakia and Hungary would be gradually withdrawn. Astonishingly, he did not expect the United States to reciprocate. The remarkable thing about this speech was that neither Gorbachev nor Shevardnadze had consulted the defence ministry before announcing the cuts. In protest, Marshal Akhromeev, Chief of the General Staff, announced his resignation the same day. He had gone along with strategic arms reductions but drew the line at conventional reductions, with America reciprocating. Gorbachev was engaged in a high wire act with his own military.

Gorbachev used the UN forum to elucidate his view of universal human values. He stressed that freedom of choice was a universal principle. Many wondered if this also extended to eastern Europe. Afterwards, he met President Reagan and President-elect George Bush on Governors Island. The Armenian earthquake disaster intervened and Gorbachev had to cut short his visit and return to Moscow.

THE BUSH-GORBACHEV RELATIONSHIP IS SLOW TO DEVELOP

The impetus in Russian-American relations was now lost as President Bush, after assuming office in January 1989, took his time to elaborate his foreign policy priorities. Bush felt that Reagan had been too quick to deal with Moscow and had been too accommodating. This revealed the difficulty the new President was having in comprehending the sea change in Soviet foreign policy. The conservative Bush administration did not want to believe that many of its cherished beliefs about the Soviet Union were dissolving before its eyes. In May 1989 Marlon Fitzwater, the White House spokesman, dismissed Gorbachev as a 'drugstore cowboy'. But George Bush changed his mind during his extensive tour of eastern and western Europe in July 1989. Everyone pressed him to meet Mikhail Gorbachev as momentous events were taking place. The relationship eventually became very close and Gorbachev remarked, on one occasion, that it was not in the interests of the Soviet Union to diminish the role of America in the world. On some occasions he excluded his own Russian interpreter from meetings with Bush, relying entirely on the American interpreter. This behaviour was puzzling but one explanation would be that Gorbachev's foreign policy agenda could only be carried out if America shared it and continued to be the dominant world power. As one of his Russian communist critics has pointed out, this was a strange policy for a Soviet leader to be pursuing.

The turning point in the relationship between James Baker, who had succeeded George Shultz as Secretary of State, and Eduard Shevardnadze, occurred in September 1989, when Shevardnadze accepted Baker's invitation to accompany him to his ranch at Jackson Hole, Wyoming [2]. Before leaving Moscow, Shevardnadze had given vent to his frustration at the tardiness of Washington's response to Russian arms proposals. Shevardnadze stayed two weeks and developed as close a relationship with Baker as he had had with Shultz. On arrival the Soviet Foreign Minister was presented with a ten-gallon Stetson. Enquiries at the Soviet embassy in Washington had failed to elicit information about the size of Shevardnadze's head, so the Americans had worked it out for themselves. The dashing Georgian cut quite a figure in his ten-gallon hat, cowboy boots and three-piece suit.

To underline the economic crisis back home, Shevardnadze had brought along Nikolai Shmelev, a pro-market economist who had published some devastating analyses of the Soviet economy. The minister was desperate for a partnership with America, whatever the cost. Without gaining anything in return, he intimated that Moscow was willing to sign a START treaty. He confirmed that the giant Krasnoyarsk radar station contravened the ABM treaty. He had hinted at this in a speech to the UN in 1986, it was only now that action could be taken as the Soviet military were reluctant to give it up. Gorbachev was later to inform Bush that he had decommissioned Krasnoyarsk in order to 'make things easier for the President'. Krasnoyarsk was not a satellite tracking station, as the Russians had been claiming for years, but a sophisticated battle management radar in a potentially anti-ballistic missile system. On his return to Moscow, he made other concessions. He accepted Washington's demand that it be permitted 880 submarine-launched Cruise missiles. Akhromeev, now an adviser to Gorbachev, and others berated him for not having gained reciprocity on this issue.

The Malta summit, in December 1989, did not produce any tangible agreements but was a major step forward in Russian-American relations. In Washington in July 1989, Akhromeev was handed a note from Bush for Gorbachev suggesting a meeting in December. The proposal was not made known at the time as the administration was having difficulty in agreeing its policy on arms control.

Shevardnadze advised Gorbachev in November 1989 that it was very important to get Bush's 'public commitment to the reform programme' and warned him that Bush was an 'indecisive leader' [13 p. 634]. Bush made up his mind about perestroika before he arrived in Malta on 1 December: it was a good idea. He had a raft of proposals about economic co-operation. The Americans had warned Gorbachev about trying to outsmart Bush at their first meeting by launching a series of new initiatives. Reykjavik obviously still smarted.

Gorbachev understood Bush to be offering an economic partnership, although he soon demonstrated that he had a woolly understanding of a market economy. There were informal agreements on eastern Europe, Germany and the Baltic republics. Eastern Europe did not present a problem because Gorbachev and Shevardnadze had reiterated, on several occasions, that the Russians would not use military force to prevent the peoples there deciding their own fate. Gorbachev said he hoped the Warsaw Pact would continue. Bush countered by saying that as long as force was not used the US would not seek to embarrass the Soviet Union in the region.

On Germany, Gorbachev counselled caution since no one in Russia favoured reunification in the short term. On the Baltic republics, he said he was willing to consider any form of association but not separation. Bush made it clear that the use of force there would be disastrous for their relationship, but otherwise the US again promised not to make life difficult for Moscow there. Rumours circulated that a deal had been struck. Moscow would accept German reunification if the US stayed out of eastern Europe and the Baltic. No such agreement was reached, much to the relief of these areas.

On arms, it was agreed to work towards the signing of a conventional forces in Europe (CFE) treaty, in 1990. A START treaty might be ready for signing at the next proposed summit, in Washington, in mid-1990. There were also sharp disagreements. Bush was critical of Soviet arms deliveries to Latin America and the behaviour of their ally, Cuba. Gorbachev retorted that he had kept his promise not to supply arms to Nicaragua. On Cuba, Gorbachev thought that the best solution was for the President to meet Fidel Castro face to face and offered to arrange a meeting. Bush brushed this aside contemptuously. Gorbachev took umbrage at Bush's assertion that western values were prevailing. This implied, responded Gorbachev, that Russia was caving in to western norms. He preferred the term 'universal, democratic values'. Eventually, they agreed to say democratic values. Malta was a watershed in Russian-American relations. Gorbachev assured Bush that he, as other Russians, did not consider America the enemy any more. Shevardnadze put it graphically. The superpowers had 'buried the Cold War at the bottom of the Mediterranean' [4 p. 165].

GORBACHEV AND EUROPE: OUR COMMON HOME

Gorbachev came up with the expression 'Europe is our common home' (the concept was elastic; it also included the US and Canada) in Paris, in February 1986, during his first official visit to western Europe after taking office. He chose France because it was a nuclear power. It would be a feather in his cap if he could interest the French in a nuclear-free world, but President Mitterrand proved quite unresponsive. When Mitterrand visited Moscow in July 1986, he confided to Gorbachev that he opposed the whole idea of SDI, which he viewed as accelerating the arms race, whereas policy should be aimed at reducing arsenals. After the Reykjavik summit, however, the French repeated their commitment to nuclear deterrence, disappointing Gorbachev.

In April 1987, in Prague, Gorbachev floated his pan-European idea but found little response from the leaders of western Europe. They preferred to take a lead from the Americans. When the British Prime Minister, Margaret Thatcher, visited Moscow in March 1987, she forcefully reiterated her commitment to nuclear deterrence (nuclear weapons have been invented, you cannot de-invent them) and her belief that the goal of the Soviet Union was to extend communism worldwide. Nevertheless, the two leaders got on extremely well as Mrs Thatcher enjoyed a good argument. As she had the ear of President Reagan, it was important for Gorbachev to attempt to win her over to his way of thinking. She was enthusiastic about something else: perestroika.

Although President Mitterrand regarded Reagan's belief in SDI as bordering on the mystical, he maintained a hard line on France's nuclear deterrent. It was non-negotiable. The French parliament even voted to upgrade their armed forces. In Moscow, in April 1987, Mrs Thatcher also confirmed her belief in the nuclear deterrent [Doc. 15].

In December 1987 Gorbachev dropped in on Mrs Thatcher en route to the Washington summit to sign the INF treaty. Geoffrey Howe, the British Foreign Secretary, was very impressed by their work rate. He compared them to two star Stakhanovites (exemplary Russian shock workers). Gorbachev's first extended official visit to Britain, in April 1989, found Mrs Thatcher passionately interested in the development of perestroika. When Gorbachev commented that many in the west were having their doubts about it, she brushed this aside and assured him that all in the west were enthusiastic about it.

After visiting France and Britain, the two west European nuclear states, it was time for Gorbachev to visit West Germany, in June 1989. The Germans had been feeling left out of the Soviet leader's diplomacy. When Kohl saw Gorbachev at Chernenko's funeral, the new Soviet leader enquired where the Federal Republic was drifting? He used the verb *driftovat*, to drift, which is not in any Russian dictionary. Kohl was probably the first western statesman to be treated to such neologisms – Gorbachev loved to pepper his remarks with newly mastered English expressions. Kohl found Gorbachev's communicative skills brilliant and attempted to pay him a compliment. Unfortunately, he likened him to Josef Goebbels, the silver-tongued Nazi propagandist. That soured relations for a while. In July, in Paris, Gorbachev told the French that the post war era was over. At the Sorbonne he underlined that pure intellect without morality constituted a terrible danger. He was in Helsinki in October, then went to Italy in November. The reception he received in Milan was the most emotional of his career. Everywhere he was feted as if he were the first man from Mars. On 1 December he became the first Soviet leader to enter the Vatican and informed Pope John Paul II that democracy was not enough, morality was also essential.

GERMANY UNITES

When West German President Richard von Weizsäcker visited Moscow in June 1987, he touched on the question of German reunification very tactfully. Gorbachev made it clear to him that it was premature to consider such a thing and even harmful to raise the issue. Gorbachev's visit to East Berlin in October 1989 brought home to him the gravity of the situation in the GDR. On 1 November Egon Krenz, the new Party leader, met Gorbachev in the Kremlin to beg for aid. Krenz stated that if East German living standards had to rely exclusively on the GDR economy, they would drop by at least 30 per cent, a political impossibility. Gorbachev told him the Soviet Union could offer little aid as Soviet republics were demanding higher prices for their raw materials. Disappointed at hearing this, Krenz then touched on the common European home. He wanted to know what place in it Russia envisaged for the GDR. He pointed out that the Soviet Union was the father of the GDR and that 'paternity for the child had to be accepted'. Gorbachev explained that the Soviet Union was forging closer links with West Germany and Bonn expected Soviet backing for German unification. All he could advise was for the GDR to foster closer relations with Bonn.

After the Berlin Wall went down in November 1989, Chancellor Kohl launched a ten-point plan for German reunification. He did not consult his Foreign Minister, Hans-Dietrich Genscher, or even his allies. Genscher, in Moscow in December, had to defend a document, parts of which he disagreed with. The meeting was tense and painful for both Genscher and Gorbachev. When Hans Modrow, the GDR Prime Minister, saw Gorbachev in January 1990, he confessed that it would probably be impossible to save the GDR. Gorbachev and his advisers had reached the same conclusion a few days earlier. The Soviet Union would take the initiative to set up a group of six: the four victorious allies – Russia, America, Britain and France – and the two German states.

When James Baker met Gorbachev in February 1990, he was at pains to stress that the US was not seeking any advantage from these developments. Next Gorbachev saw Kohl and told him that it was up to the Germans to decide things for themselves. Gorbachev hoped for a neutral, united Germany, but Kohl, now full of self-confidence, rejected this and proposed that Germany should join NATO. In March the Alliance for Germany, backed by Kohl's own party, won the East German elections. In April the new government proposed that unification be achieved according to the federal constitution. The GDR would simply be integrated into West Germany and thereby disappear. In May the GDR signed the state treaty with the Federal Republic on economic, monetary and social unity. The Deutsche Mark (DM) became the common currency on 1 July.

The reunification of Germany on 3 October 1990 resulted from the coming together of three factors: the Gorbachev revolution in the Soviet Union, the collapse of the GDR economy which led to large numbers of its citizens making for West Germany, and George Bush's determination to make German unity one of the crowning achievements of his presidency. Gorbachev simply conceded everything the man in the White House wanted. On the important issue of whether a united Germany should be a member of NATO, pressure from Bush and Baker led eventually to Gorbachev giving in, orally, to the consternation of his officials. In his memoirs, Gorbachev claims that the decision to allow Germans to decide their own security arrangements – it was a foregone conclusion that they would vote for NATO – originated with him, and not Bush. The White House sees it the other way round. One of the reasons for the acceptance of Germany in NATO was Kohl's close personal relationship with Gorbachev.

A striking example of this took place at Archys, in the north Caucasus, in July 1990. Here, in formal and informal meetings, the two leaders agreed many of the details of reunification. Without consulting Shevardnadze, who had done all the spade work on Soviet-German relations, Gorbachev abandoned all claims as an occupying power and any restriction on German sovereignty. He agreed to the withdrawal of Russian forces, with the Germans promising to build accommodation in the Soviet Union for the returning personnel. The Germans also paid for the troops to leave. Had Gorbachev not been so desperate for German financial aid, he could have struck a much more profitable bargain. German unification, and the Soviet terms for it, were not discussed in the Politburo. Shevardnadze was unhappy as he was aware that the ire of the military and the conservatives would descend upon him for 'losing' the GDR [71].

GORBACHEV AND EASTERN EUROPE

Gorbachev met the east European leaders after Chernenko's funeral in March 1985, and explained that the Brezhnev doctrine was dead. Henceforth, they could choose their own leaders and policies. This was reiterated at a meeting of the Warsaw Pact in April 1985. Gorbachev, of course, assumed that eastern Europeans had made their choice. They had chosen socialism and would never go back on this. Reform, therefore, in these countries would be socialist and would enhance the appeal of socialism world-wide.

The Brezhnev leadership had ruled out military intervention in 1981, when the Polish military took over. This remained the Politburo's policy. It had invested too much in the peace process to throw it away by invading Poland. In March 1989 the Hungarian Party leader, Károly Grósz, in Moscow, explained why Hungary had introduced a multi-party system. There was not a murmur of protest as it was considered a Hungarian internal affair. In July 1989 the communists were defeated in Poland in elections and the way was clear for a non-communist Prime Minister to take office.

Also in July, Gorbachev, at the Council of Europe, stated: 'Any interference in domestic affairs of any kind, any attempts to limit the sovereignty of states, both of friends and allies, no matter whose it is, is impermissible'. In October 1989, attending the 40th anniversary celebrations of the GDR, Gorbachev and the communist leader, Erich Honecker, did not see eye to eye. East Germans called on Gorbachev to save them. He told East Berliners that history punishes those who are left behind. Honecker departed and was replaced by Egon Krenz, but the latter was quite incapable of coping with the disintegration of the GDR. Gorbachev was not the only one who believed that the East Germans would remain within the socialist camp: the West German Social Democratic Party (SPD) also advised him that this would happen. The SPD was taken aback by the calls for reunification and most members opposed it. Only Willy Brandt, among SPD leaders, caught the public mood and supported the disappearance of the East German state. When the Berlin Wall came down on 9 November 1989, it was the end of post-war politics. Revolution rolled over eastern Europe like an irresistible tide. It washed away four decades of communist rule as the people rejected Russian-style socialism. In Czechoslovakia, it was called the velvet revolution. No one had to die for freedom. Some blood was, however, spilt in Romania: Nicolae and Elena Ceauşescu, the hated dictators, were summarily tried and shot on Christmas Day 1989.

GORBACHEV AND CHINA

Gorbachev's visit to China in May 1989 had tragic consequences. Soviet reforms had aroused great interest among Chinese youth and many of them dared to hope that democracy, unknown in China's history, could take root there. Economic success was breeding optimism. Gorbachev's visit was a triumph for him and he was feted as a hero by masses of Chinese demonstrators. However, this adulation of a foreign leader deeply embarrassed the ageing Chinese leadership. They and Gorbachev agreed to normalise relations between the two neighbours and not to intervene in one another's internal affairs. The Gorbachev visit added impetus to the democracy movement in China and led to the decision by Deng Xiaoping to use force in Tiananmen Square, in Beijing, on 4 June. The Communist Party of China feared that it was losing its grip on the country. Democracy to it meant anarchy and the possible break-up of the People's Republic. The world condemned the Chinese leadership and ostracised it for its action on 4 June. Trade, however, continued. The lesson was not lost on some Soviet and east European leaders. The GDR openly applauded the brutal suppression of unarmed civilians.

GORBACHEV'S DOMESTIC DIFFICULTIES CAUSE PROBLEMS FOR BUSH

Gorbachev and Bush maintained regular contact and the US ambassador, Jack Matlock, a fluent Russian speaker, saw the Soviet leader regularly. One of the most contentious issues was Gorbachev's nationality policy. The US did not want to promote the break-up of the Soviet Union and made it clear to the republics, especially those in the Baltic – Estonia, Latvia and Lithuania – that it would not support their drive for independence. American policy was to support Gorbachev in his efforts to transform the Soviet Union into a democratic federation. Washington also made no secret about seeing a liberal market economy as the solution to the travails of the Russian command economy.

The Russian Federation posed a bigger problem for Washington. The American ambassador cultivated good relations with Boris Yeltsin and Russian democrats, and official American policy was to encourage Gorbachev and Yeltsin to work closely together. A postcommunist, democratic Soviet Union, headed by Gorbachev and Yeltsin, was the dream ticket. Unfortunately Yeltsin had other ideas. Gorbachev found it very difficult to accept criticism, especially from Russian democrats.

Gorbachev and Yeltsin had fallen out in November 1987, when Yeltsin had been unceremoniously dumped as Party leader in the city of Moscow. When the Russian Supreme Soviet, the new parliament, was elected in the spring of 1990, he became chair or speaker, and this constitutionally made him head of the Russian Federation, an eventuality which Gorbachev had done his best to prevent.

When the US ambassador paid a courtesy visit on Ruslan Khasbulatov, Yeltsin's nomination as deputy speaker, in June 1990, he was astonished by what he heard. Khasbulatov informed him that the Russian Federation would soon be the successor state to the Soviet Union. There would be a union, a loose confederation, which would not need a constitution, as it would not be a state in international law. Economic decision-making would rest with the republics. The

Russian Federation wanted to move towards a market economy but the central Soviet bureaucracy was hindering this. It wanted its diplomats in Soviet embassies abroad and would eventually conduct its own foreign economic relations. Eventually Soviet embassies would become Russian embassies, as the Russian Federation would be the successor state. Conventional military forces would be under the command of the republics, nuclear forces would be run from the centre. This was an astonishing scenario, given that Yeltsin was forever swearing allegiance to the federal or confederal goal proposed by Gorbachev. Now his deputy was informing the US that his real goal was a very loose confederation, dominated by Russia. Since Gorbachev stood in the way, he would be destroyed. Since the above is remarkably close to what actually did happen in December 1991, it is tempting to see Yeltsin playing a double game. However, had it not been for the attempted coup in August 1991, the plan might not have come to fruition.

Khasbulatov's vision of the future was not what the US administration wanted to hear. The Americans found Yeltsin difficult to deal with, mainly because he acted on instinct when taking some key decisions. He also lacked the charm and suave demeanour of Gorbachev. Since, presumably, Khasbulatov's office had been bugged by the KGB, Gorbachev was soon apprised of the conversation. On occasions when Bush encouraged Gorbachev to work more closely with Yeltsin, he would counter that he regarded Yeltsin as a 'destroyer' [54].

In the spring of 1990, the state planning commission, Gosplan, recommended that the country move towards a market economy, although there was considerable confusion about what a market economy entailed. However, many leading economic officials, especially in the military-industrial complex, quickly decided they were not in favour, as it would weaken their position. The battle raged during the summer but eventually a plan was proposed for the economy to move to the market in 500 days, the so-called 500-day programme, authored by Academician Shatalin and Grigory Yavlinsky. There was also a counter variant, a much more modest approach, proposed by Prime Minister Nikolai Ryzhkov and Academician Abalkin. Gorbachev invited the two groups to negotiate a compromise but this was like mixing chalk and cheese. Gorbachev could not make up his mind and the radical proposal lapsed. As a consequence, he moved politically to the right from the autumn of 1990 to the spring of 1991.

It was during this period that the tragic events in Vilnius, in

Lithuania, occurred. In January 1991 tension between Moscow and Vilnius escalated and Gorbachev sent the Lithuanians an ultimatum: either retreat from their goal of independence or face the consequences. Shortly thereafter Moscow's troops stormed the radio and TV centre and the TV tower, leaving 13 dead. Gorbachev denied he had given instructions to attack and shed blood. The US deplored the deaths but accepted Gorbachev's assurances that he had not been the butcher. Washington appealed for a political solution and warned that the use of force would seriously jeopardise relations between the two states. A week later, Moscow's forces attacked the Latvian Ministry of Affairs' building in Riga, killing four persons. Again Gorbachev denied complicity. It turned out that a local officer had acted on his own initiative. This brought into doubt Gorbachev's control of his military and police. The west took a lenient line because it was engaged in the Gulf War and needed Gorbachev on board.

THE GULF WAR LEADS TO JOINT SUPERPOWER POLICY

Sadam Hussein's invasion of Kuwait on 1 August 1990, and its incorporation in Iraq, was a severe test for the evolving Soviet-American relationship. Gorbachev faced a dilemma: Iraq was an ally and there were thousands of Russian troops in the country. James Baker and Eduard Shevardnadze met at Vnukovo 2 airport in Moscow and agreed on a statement condemning the Iraqi aggression – the precursor of joint votes in the UN. On 9 September Gorbachev and Bush met in Helsinki and talked most of the day. The Soviet leader wanted assurances on two points: that military pressure would be used against Saddam Hussein, without escalating into war, and that US forces would leave Kuwait after it was liberated.

Gorbachev asked about the possibility of US financial aid for Russia. He was obliquely hinting that Kuwait and credits were linked. After the tragic events in Vilnius, Bush made it clear that further use of force would make it impossible for America to help economically. Gorbachev assured Bush he was aware of this but, in his judgement, the Soviet Union was on the brink of civil war. The Soviet leader kept his promise, made in Helsinki, that the Soviet Union would co-operate with the United States in ensuring that Iraqi aggression did not reap any rewards.

GORBACHEV'S PROBLEMS MOUNT

President Bush was due in Moscow for a summit in February 1991, but tension in the Baltic republics made it impossible to travel. There was also the fact that the Soviet military were not observing the conventional forces in Europe (CFE) treaty, agreed in Paris in November 1990. One ruse was to transfer tanks behind the Urals, in Asia, to prevent them being destroyed. Another was to arm the navy with some tanks. It appeared that Gorbachev would not or could not rein in his military. General Moiseev, Chief of the General Staff, was dispatched to Washington to iron out the misunderstandings.

In March 1991 James Baker dropped in to see Gorbachev in Moscow. The Soviet leader then informed him that he had received information from one of Yeltsin's associates: the Russian leader had approached the United States, wanting to know what the US reaction would be if he took power by unconstitutional means. This revelation was news to Baker and he managed to convince Gorbachev that no such approach had been made. How could Yeltsin take power with the KGB and the military on Gorbachev's side? It was disinformation, fabricated by the KGB. This was another instance of Gorbachev giving too much credence to KGB reporting. The KGB chief, Vladimir Kryuchkov, consistently argued that a state of emergency was needed to restore order. He also negatively assessed American initiatives, seeing them as a US attempt to undermine his country. The trouble with Kryuchkov was that he actually believed much of the disinformation he was showering on Gorbachev.

In May 1991 the US ambassador was surprised, during one of his meetings with Gorbachev, to be treated to a plaintive monologue. The gist of the flood of words was that the President feared that President Bush was preparing to change his policy towards the Soviet Union. It was quite clear that Gorbachev desperately needed Bush's support and he also needed money. The ambassador had asked for his tour of duty to end and Gorbachev pointedly asked him if he thought the Soviet ship of state was about to sink? The next day Gorbachev met Rupert Murdoch, the media magnate. He was even more pessimistic and told him that Bush was risking a new Cold War. This stung the President into action. He caressed Gorbachev with warm words of empathy and assured him that the thought of cooling their relationship had never entered his head. Progress was made on the CFE treaty and it could be sent to the Senate. In June Gorbachev was informed that America would grant the Soviet Union a much-needed credit of US$1.5 billion to purchase grain.

This was fine but much more was needed. Every foreign statesman he met was informed that the Gulf War had cost US$100 billion. The money had been instantly found. Why could such a sum not be raised to support perestroika? After all, it was ten or a hundred times more important for the world than the Gulf War. The rich man's club was the Group of Seven (G7). Could the Soviet Union possibly join? In order to get an invitation, he needed a financial plan.

The ideal person to draw one up was Grigory Yavlinsky. He went off to Harvard to work with Graham Allison. Yavlinsky called the joint effort 'the window of opportunity', Allison described it as 'the great design'. Gorbachev pulled out all the stops and invited Mrs Thatcher to his Moscow dacha. She was completely won over and instructed the US ambassador to send a message to the President: he was to lead the western initiative to save Gorbachev. When Matlock pointed out that this would be difficult since Gorbachev had yet to adopt market reforms, she brushed his words aside and told him to think like a statesman, not as a diplomat, trying to avoid doing anything.

On 17 June 1991 Valentin Pavlov, the Prime Minister, requested parliament to confer on him some extraordinary powers, mainly on economic policy. He had not cleared it first with the President. On 20 June Gavriil Popov, the newly elected mayor of Moscow, paid a farewell visit on the US ambassador, who was soon to return to Washington. Popov scribbled on a piece of paper that a coup was being organised to remove Gorbachev. News about this had to be got to Yeltsin, at the time in America. Matlock asked for the names. They were Pavlov, Kryuchkov, Yazov, Lukyanov. (They turned out to be the attempted coup leaders, in August 1991.) The ambassador then informed Gorbachev that President Bush had information about an attempt to remove him. Gorbachev thanked the President for his concern but said he had everything under control. Bush then phoned Gorbachev and revealed that the source had been Popov. Now the KGB knew who had blown the whistle on them. Bush decided not to name the alleged conspirators but this may have been a mistake. Gorbachev, apparently, thought they were a group of conservative deputies in parliament.

Gorbachev's bid for G7 money was doomed from the outset. President Bush had thought that he had made it clear to the Soviet leader that only a programme which clearly mapped out the steps to a market economy would be likely to succeed in London, in July. On 31 May Bush and Baker met Vladimir Shcherbakov, Deputy Prime Minister, and Evgeny Primakov, head of foreign economic relations in the Security Council. The US President concluded that Gorbachev did not have a viable programme. Yavlinsky was not consulted. Gorbachev reasoned that, as the reform programme had to be implemented by the government, it should draft it. In London, everyone listened politely to Gorbachev and there was little reaction to his invitation to business leaders to invest in the Soviet Union, but no money was promised by the G7. Gorbachev asked for, and was granted, membership of the International Monetary Fund (IMF), an international body concerned with macroeconomics. Gorbachev was dejected by his first major foreign policy failure since Soviet-American relations had become friendly.

He took out his ire on Bush on 17 July. In a long, rambling speech he complained about not knowing what the United States expected of the Soviet Union. How was the Soviet Union to develop? What did George Bush want from him? Again he mentioned US$100 million as the sum the Gulf War had cost and which had been found easily. Why could a similar amount not be made available for the project of the century? President Bush was offended by these remarks and coldly apologised for not having made himself clear before. He reiterated the American wish that the Soviet Union become a democratic state with a market economy, integrated in the western world. Again he stated that America did not want the political and economic ruin of the Soviet Union. What is remarkable about Gorbachev's words is that Bush had repeated, time and again, what America wanted from the Soviet Union. He made a poor impression on Bush, who began wondering if Gorbachev was beginning to lose his grip on reality. The reasons for his *faux pas* may have been his total inability to grasp what a market economy entailed and KGB analyses which stressed that America was trying to destroy Russia.

THE LAST SUMMIT

George Bush arrived in Moscow in July 1991 for his first Moscow summit as President. It was to be the fourth, and last, Bush–Gorbachev meeting. Ironically, it was the most rewarding for both leaders, on a purely personal basis. The START treaty was ready for signature, after ten years of hard negotiations; the CFE treaty was with the senate for ratification; a bill was before Congress conferring on the Soviet Union most favoured nation status; and there was a tentative agreement on a Middle East peace conference. However, the realities of the domestic situation impinged on the meeting. A note was passed to Bush, informing him that six Lithuanian customs officials had been killed during the night. Gorbachev was embarrassed as this was the first he had heard of the incident. It appeared that the incident had been staged by the Ministry of Internal Affairs to disrupt the summit. It also demonstrated that Bush was better informed about Soviet domestic events than President Gorbachev. Gorbachev, it seemed, was not in full control of his police.

The growing influence of the republics was marked by Gorbachev's invitation to Yeltsin and Nazarbaev, the leader of Kazakhstan, to join him in a working lunch and to participate in some of the sessions. Yeltsin replied that he preferred to meet Bush face to face, President to President, in his office. He kept Bush waiting ten minutes and the meeting overran. The Americans were not amused. At the official dinner Yeltsin tried to upstage Gorbachev. When Barbara Bush entered he attempted to escort her to the top table, as if he were the host.

In planning his itinerary, Bush had been advised by American diplomats to visit Kiev, the capital of Ukraine. Initially the Soviet Ministry of Foreign Affairs raised no objection, but then it changed its mind and advised Bush against travelling to Kiev, given the tense situation there. Instead, he could spend time with Gorbachev in Stavropol krai. Evidently, Gorbachev was piqued by Bush's wish to visit Ukraine at a time when the Ukrainians were proving difficult during negotiations on a new Union treaty. In Kiev, President Bush was to meet the constitutional head of the republic, Leonid Kravchuk. All toasts were to be in Ukrainian and English. No Russian was to be used. Bush advised the Ukrainians to concentrate on developing democracy before aiming for independence and to avoid the pitfalls of nationalism. Their future lay as part of the new Union Gorbachev was forging. They turned a deaf ear to this advice. Bush's words were dubbed, disrespectfully, his chicken Kiev speech.

THE ATTEMPTED COUP AND AFTER

The attempted coup in August 1991 was a devastating blow for Gorbachev. He felt betrayed since the coup leaders were all his own men. President Bush, when he met the press, was defensive and gave the impression that the coup had been successful and that he would have to deal with the coup leaders. They seized upon this and broadcast it repeatedly on the Soviet media. Bush declined to phone Yeltsin. That evening he changed his mind and declared the attempted coup illegal and unconstitutional. He then phoned Yeltsin. One of the reasons for the lack of clarity in the US position was that Jack Matlock, the very able ambassador, had returned to Washington. He was not consulted but on television declared that the coup was bound to fail. President Mitterrand began to refer to the 'new leaders' of the Soviet Union.

The failed coup transformed the Gorbachev–Yeltsin relationship. The Russian leader was now in the driving seat and unsophisticated in bringing this home to the Soviet President. He displayed a nice turn of phrase when he phoned Gorbachev, in the Crimea, at the end of the coup: he enquired if the Soviet leader were still alive. He then told him that George and Barbara Bush had been in contact and that they sent their greeting. The couple had been praying for everyone for three days.

America and the west hoped that Gorbachev could salvage a Union of Sovereign States from the wreckage of the Soviet Union. They preferred to deal with one central authority with control over nuclear weapons rather than four nuclear powers: Russia, Belarus, Ukraine and Kazakhstan. The G7 went through the motions of arranging a loan to the Soviet Union. America and the west recognised the independence of the Soviet republics, such as Estonia, Latvia and Lithuania. The Gorbachevian world was finally shattered in December 1991, when the leaders of Russia, Belarus and Ukraine met outside Minsk, Belarus, to dissolve the Soviet Union and give birth to the Commonwealth of Independent States (CIS), a loose confederation of states. Their first move was to inform President Bush, before telling Gorbachev.

The Cold War was over and the United States had won. It was the only superpower left standing. In the shadows China was growing and will, eventually, challenge American dominance. Eastern Europe, long regarded as absolutely essential to Soviet security, just withered away. The Soviet command economy caved in before the capitalist economy of the west. Yet, the United States was not economically and socially healthy. The huge budget deficit of the Reagan years had weakened the country and the government simply did not have the resources to deal with crime, poverty, health care and unemployment. Washington was not rich enough to pay for the Gulf War alone. The Saudis and other oil rich states had to contribute. Yet US arms proved invincible. Domestically, there was a feeling of pessimism and malaise. Some commentators talked about the imperial burden slowly breaking the back of America.

The reaction to crises in the Soviet Union and United States could not have been more different. In the former, there was a lack of willingness to face up to the problems and this rendered solutions ineffective. Money-making was frowned upon. In the latter, crises were treated as challenges and stimulated great creativity. Rampant materialism held sway. Whereas in 1991 America seemed as if it could cede economic primacy eventually to Japan, by the late 1990s this appeared absurd. The US economy is in robust health, the budget deficits, ever present since 1969, have been sharply reduced, and a record number are in employment. In the late 1990s, Russia, the successor state to the Soviet Union, is still trying to turn its economy round [4, 5, 13, 15, 25, 54, 55, 58, 63].

PART THREE: ASSESSMENT

7 THE TWENTIETH CENTURY: AN OVERVIEW

Europe dominated the world in 1900 but two civil wars, the first and second world wars, destroyed that hegemony. In 1945 Russia was the major European military force but America dominated the world in the same vein as Europe in 1900. The US, in 1945, was both an economic and military power. That combination made it possible for the American political leadership to begin dreaming of a new world order which would mirror American values. Russia and America were isolationist powers until 1945, the former by force of circumstances, the latter by choice.

Russia began as an expansionist power under Lenin but the defeat of revolution in Germany in 1921 ended that dream. Afterwards, the young Soviet state concentrated on building up its domestic strength. First and foremost, this meant developing a strong industrial base. This, in turn, would make it possible to produce the armaments which would make the country secure from outside attack. Stalin's misreading of Hitler almost cost him and the Soviet Union their existence. His near fatal pact with Hitler taught him a lesson he never forgot: do not trust in alliances to guarantee Russia's security. As far as Stalin was concerned, it was once bitten, twice shy. This was to have unfortunate consequences in and after 1945 when America attempted to draw the Soviet Union into a mutually enriching relationship to guarantee the peace of the world.

The period from 1900 to 1991 can be divided into two neat halves. The first half, to May 1945, saw Russia and America never pose a threat to one another's security. America did intervene in the Russian Civil War (1918–20) but balanced this by forcing the Japanese to leave the Russian Far East afterwards. American communists did contribute to the construction of the Soviet Union, but then Henry Ford built much more. For instance, the tractor plant at Stalingrad, now Volgograd.

The second half, from May 1945 to December 1991, was full of hostility and almost erupted into nuclear war. The Cold War got under way in earnest in 1947 and lasted until the late Gorbachev era. The first two years and the last two years of this period were the most relaxed and hopeful. The 1950s, 1960s, 1970s and the first half of the 1980s, on the other hand, saw a violent ideological conflict between two empires competing for world dominance.

The world outside Europe, later to become known as the Third World, was dominated by European empires during the first half of the century. The largest was the British, then came the French, Dutch, Belgian, Portuguese, Spanish and Italian. The Japanese came on to the scene in the 1930s, when they penetrated China. All these empires collapsed after 1945. In their place appeared a plethora of new states, many of them appearing on the world stage for the first time. Most of them were not nation states but groupings of tribes or clans. They all wanted their place in the sun and to escape from imperial influence. To America, this caused some alarm. Since most of these new states were unstable, there was fertile soil for the spread of communism. To the Soviet Union, these new states presented an unprecedented opportunity. If they adopted the Leninist brand of socialism, this would serve as the demonstration effect. It would also subtract other countries from the sum of capitalist states in the world. The Third World, the periphery for the superpowers, was to pay a high price for the Cold War. Russia and America intervened in their own interests, not those of the locals [*Doc. 6*].

In 1945, economically, America and Russia not only led the world, they dominated it. In 1991 the US economy was still the largest, but other countries, the oil states of the Gulf and Japan for instance, were in front as regards wealth per head of population. Russia was in free fall and about to embark on a bumpy ride from a command to a capitalist economy. Japan, under the US nuclear umbrella and consequently able to devote little to defence, was the outstanding success story. Hong Kong, South Korea, Taiwan, Indonesia, Malaysia, Singapore and Thailand also expanded rapidly.

The great surprise was the People's Republic of China, long the victim of Mao Zedong's wrong turnings in economic policy. The great leap forward (dubbed the great leap backward by his critics), the cultural revolution, the promotion of communes as the route to agricultural growth (and disastrous espousals of the Russian Lysenko's crazy theories, such as killing all insect-eating birds) dragged China down. Fortunately for China, Deng Xiaoping won the succession struggle and market reforms began in the late 1970s. By 1991, China had registered the greatest economic expansion of any state in history, in physical terms. The Tiananmen square massacre, in June 1989, led to recentralisation and a rapid drop in growth rates in 1990–91. This experience discredited those who had advocated greater central control of the economy and led China to declare that its goal was a full market economy.

In Europe, West Germany was the star performer and by 1991 the European Union (EU) had become a major economic power in its own right. In 1996 the EU accounted for about 31 per cent of world output and 20 per cent of world trade. The US provided about 27 per cent of global production and 18 per cent of world trade. However, the US dollar, in 1996, had between 40 and 60 per cent share of world finance, far exceeding the economic weight of the US. On the other hand, the US, in the 15 years to 1996, had been running current account deficits. Its net foreign debt exceeded US$1 trillion, and it was mounting at 15 to 20 per cent annually. Only the Euro can challenge the dollar as a world currency in the twenty-first century.

Until the late 1970s, one-third of the world placed their faith in centrally planned economies. To nervous Americans it was not certain that the market economies, which entailed some level of democracy, would prevail. The tide then turned, and by 1991 the command economy model had been completely discredited. The fear of communism dissipated in the 1980s, when it became evident that the economic battle had been won. The decline of the Soviet Union in the 1980s rendered its subventioning of client states in eastern Europe and the Third World economically impossible. All collapsed except Cuba and North Korea. By the late 1990s, these two states were among the poorest in the world.

Post-war economic prosperity in the west (western Europe, north America and Japan) was based on the Bretton Woods agreement, of 1944. The main currency became the US dollar and it was placed on the gold standard. All other convertible currencies fluctuated against the US dollar. Market economies functioned in the knowledge that there was always a fall-back currency, the dollar, and a state which would not allow them to collapse, America. If one major capitalist country collapsed, the communists could take over and this could start a chain reaction which could undermine capitalism world-wide. The main loser would be the United States. Market economies accepted US dominance as the affordable price for their own well-being. The willingness of the US to open its market to foreign goods was a major factor in the rapid expansion of the EU and Japan.

In a nuclear world, only the US could guarantee the security of the west. This arrangement was to the liking of the west European powers since it meant that they could cut their defence budgets and prevail upon Washington to keep its troops and war matériel in Europe. But not all Europeans welcomed American dominance. France was the outstanding exception. General de Gaulle took France out of NATO but relied on NATO to make France secure. West European socialists bridled at the irresistible tide of American capitalism but, when in office, sought American loans.

Russia took the decision to remain outside the Bretton Woods agreement and declined to join its institutions, the IMF and World Bank. It also stayed outside the General Agreement on Tariffs and Trade (GATT). The Stalin leadership did not rate the opportunity of obtaining loans from the IMF and World Bank very highly. Trade was not of much consequence either. These decisions were, presumably, defensive. Western loans would require the divulgence of foreign currency and gold reserves, and economic growth rates, data which were treated in Moscow as state secrets. In 1945 self-confidence was high as victory over Germany appeared to have confirmed the superiority of the Soviet model over the capitalist model. The Soviet empire was expanding and the correlation of forces appeared to be moving in Moscow's favour. This was not only the view of the Stalin leadership, it was shared by anti-communist intellectuals in eastern Europe who became extremely pessimistic about the future. Once Leninist socialism descended on them, the likelihood of it being overthrown was viewed as extremely remote.

The contrast between the opportunities facing Stalin in 1945 to become a member of the world club and the desperate efforts of Gorbachev to break down its doors, is extreme. Whereas Stalin did not regard the club as capable of contributing to Soviet growth, Gorbachev saw it as the last chance saloon. Only its largesse could save the Soviet Union. Perceptions of the market changed rapidly over time. If Stalin had introduced elements of the market into the Soviet economy, arguably it would have made it more effective, but he equated the market economy with capitalism, therefore a cancer.

The Chinese leadership, on the other hand, in the late 1970s, regarded the market and capitalism as separate entities. It viewed the market and socialism as quite compatible. The main reason may be that the Chinese, in the late 1970s, were in dire economic straits, and adopted the only other successful model available – capitalism. Hong Kong may have been the catalyst. In the late 1970s, the British colony was prosperous, but Britain did not permit any democracy at that time. The Hong Kong Chinese appeared to prove that a flourishing market economy could develop under authoritarian rule. The

Russians had nothing similar to contemplate at the end of the war. In 1945 Stalin wished to impose his authority again over the Soviet Union in order to rebuild it quickly. The most effective way of doing this, he reasoned, was to have strong central government and central planning.

The Vietnam War weakened the US economically. It came off the gold standard and began to run up larger and larger budget deficits. The latter were financed, increasingly, by selling government bonds to the Japanese and anyone who would buy them. The Japanese began to run up huge trade surpluses with the US. Washington tried to cope with this unsettling phenomenon by appealing to the Japanese to restrict their exports and to open up their market to US exports. However, Japanese consumers preferred Japanese goods. The budget deficits, the largest in history, meant the US could not finance the Gulf War out of its own resources. It had to prevail on the Saudis and other rich Arab states to help to foot the bill. This graphically underlined the transformation of America's fortunes.

Paradoxically, at a time when it was struggling economically, it was militarily dominant. This was not due to the number of troops or military vehicles but the advanced technological equipment it was able to deploy. Militarily, the US was preeminent in 1991, but politically and economically, it was losing ground. The bipolar world of 1945 had become the multipolar world of 1991.

SOURCES OF HOSTILITY BETWEEN THE SUPERPOWERS

What are the sources of the hostility which marked relations between Russia and America from the mid-1940s to the mid-1980s?

*   The decision of the US administration to play a global role after 1945, for the first time. The wealth and power of America permitted it to contemplate this role. It would make the world safe for democracy by establishing a new world order.

*   The ideological drive of both states; both regarded their destiny as shaping the world in their image.

*   The imperative of security.

If the US had decided, in 1945, to retreat to the Americas and leave the rest of the world to its own devices, as in 1919, the Cold War would not have emerged. There would have been no competition and tension between Russia and America. The US, secure in the knowledge that it would be extremely difficult for any power to invade and conquer the country, would have been content merely to trade with the rest of the world.

The reason it decided to play a world role was due to the politicians and diplomats who held sway at the time. They were European specialists and they concluded that it was America's withdrawal from Europe after the First World War which prepared the ground for the rise of Hitler and fascism. The same applied to the Far East, with the rise of Japanese military imperialism. European economic weakness in the 1920s had contributed to the Great Depression, beginning in 1929. There was a real chance that capitalism would not survive the 1930s. Roosevelt's New Deal saved America but it meant Washington had no time or energy for the rest of the world. It paid a heavy price for this insouciance. A major reason why the European economies did not prosper were the barriers to trade. Each state concentrated on autarchy, to husband its foreign and gold reserves, and, in so doing, exacerbated the general economic situation. For instance, the British practised imperial preference, trading with the empire at the expense of comparable goods.

The Bretton Woods agreement signified that the US was willing to take on the role of the world's banker. As America was the leading world economy, it naturally favoured free trade and stable foreign exchange rates. This made risk management easier. The states of the United States had the same currency and traded freely with one another. However, the US did not always observe free trade. Prohibition is an example, but that disastrous attempt at regulatin̲g alcohol intake had proved the point. The Americans were con̲vince̲d that they had arrived at the most successful political and economic model of all time – American democracy.

All the rest of the world needed to do in order to become as rich as America was to copy them. This implied a liberal political and economic order. Since the US was a strong state and was rich, it needed weak (small may be a better term) government. But it needed a strong state to project its influence abroad. Hence the US was against empires, imperial preference, closed clubs, military rule, indeed rule by small elites. Americans believed that the benefits of the market economy would not ripen without democracy. Time has revealed, however, that strong economic growth can be achieved without democracy. Some American policy-makers felt a moral responsibility to bring the gifts of the American experience to the great unwashed. Those with religious convictions also felt morally bound to help the needy.

Roosevelt and Truman were against zones of influence as they undermined the above scenario for world development. However, in practice, they were willing to concede that the Soviets had a right to protect their security on their western borders. East European governments should not engage in anti-Russian policies. Had Russian occupation policy been as benign in eastern Europe as in Finland then the tensions might have been resolved. As Soviet suspiciousness grew, to them the new world order meant their political demise and they took measures to increase their country's security in eastern Europe. This, in turn, made the Americans anxious. A vicious circle came into existence: every move to enhance one side's security was perceived as a threat by the other. This, inevitably, led to counter measures and snowballed into the Cold War. Each side presented its moves as defensive but was perceived by the other as offensive. This underlines the fact that mutual trust had evaporated. This phenomenon can also be called the security dilemma.

WHY DID AMERICA COME TO GUARANTEE WEST EUROPEAN SECURITY?

West European political parties (except in Britain) felt insecure when faced with communist parties. The authority of the Soviet Union was great and communists argued that German fascism had buried capitalism. Private ownership of the means of production had led to war; public ownership was more equitable and would prevent war. It would also guarantee a rising standard of living for working people. Free elections could bring communists to power. The dilemma was more severe for Britain. Economically, it could no longer play its imperial role and appealed to the United States to take over the burden in Greece and the Middle East. West European government needed large loans from Washington. If the Americans were not generous, they could be faced with a rapidly expanding communist sphere of influence and the military budget would then have to rise.

The Truman administration sympathised with the west Europeans but Congress would not foot the bill. The tactic adopted was to exaggerate the threat of Soviet expansionism. Washington was aware that Moscow had no intention of invading western Europe but had to frighten legislators with the prospect. The Marshall Plan and the Truman doctrine were the result. Funds were provided for Greece, Turkey and western Europe. Washington learnt two lessons from this experience. The first was that the President, to get his way, needed to summon up a crisis by exaggerating the Soviet threat. Second, since

Congress would always jib at increasing budget spending, covert means had to be developed to raise funds. The communist take-over in Czechoslovakia in February 1948, and the Berlin blockade which began in June 1948, were like self-fulfilling prophesies to the Truman administration. In reality, there were no Soviet troops in Czechoslovakia and the Czechoslovak communists took power themselves, partly due to the lack of political skill of the social democrats. The west, however, saw the whole episode as being manipulated by the Kremlin.

The Berlin blockade was to prevent the introduction of the Deutsche Mark and the inevitable West German state. It was defensive but Stalin revealed a startling lack of finesse in his handling of the situation. Early on, he could have secured an agreement on favourable terms to himself but declined. The astonishing thing is that the longer the blockade lasted the more likely a West German state was to come into existence. It also gave credence to Truman's analysis of Soviet intentions. Stalin was very slow to react to this. The formation of the Federal Republic in 1949, and, as a counter, the GDR, divided Germany and Europe until 1989. Stalin's policies had led to his worst case scenario coming into existence – a divided Germany in the western camp which would eventually join NATO.

Access to Soviet archives, since 1991, has thrown little light on Stalin's maladroit diplomacy. But they have revealed that Stalin's advisers in Germany had not anticipated the airlift and, once it was underway, thought that it would fail. The Berlin blockade made east–west relations adversarial and poisoned Berlin relations until 1990. Time and again Khrushchev returned to the Berlin problem in an effort to make up for Stalin's failure in 1948–49. The Berlin blockade also promoted the establishment of NATO. West Europeans felt insecure and appealed to the Americans to retain their military presence and to guarantee the security of the region. Only the US could do this, as it was a nuclear power. The Marshall Plan and the Truman doctrine were tangible successes for west European lobbying. It was the weakness of the region which led to the Americans playing a vital role in the economic development and security. The Marshall Plan kick-started the west European economies and an extraordinary growth of the region got under way until the 1970s. Britain obtained the largest share of Marshall Aid, but it was West Germany which benefited most, as it retooled its industries.

The US nuclear monopoly lasted four years, until 1949, when the Russians successfully tested their first atomic bomb. Now Soviet capabilities, rather than intentions, had to be considered very seriously.

Truman was obliged to give the go-ahead for the development of a US hydrogen bomb. The adoption of NSC-68 underlined the American determination to retain their ascendancy. This then became the pattern for the next 40 years between the superpowers. A technical advance by one side had to be countered by the other and this promoted the spiral of arms production. It was also a period of considerable anxiety as neither side could rest assured that it had achieved security. This can be called the spiral of angst. The Russians were always very concerned about Germany. Their policies directly contributed to the establishment of a West German state, its rearmament and integration in NATO. West Germany, with nuclear weapons, was a nightmare which never materialised. Given the proximity of the Soviet Union to western Europe and the distance between it and the United States, it was inevitable that the Americans would come to depend more and more on the nuclear deterrent. Conventional superiority over time was conceded to the Russians but high technology and nuclear weapons rendered this of less and less significance. The Middle East wars were useful testing grounds for Soviet equipment and it was often found wanting. This was an added reason for prudence on the Soviet side.

WHY DID RUSSIA AND AMERICA GRADUALLY BECOME SYSTEMIC RIVALS?

Russia and America competed with one another as systems. The systems can be perceived as communism and capitalism, freedom and tyranny, the command economy versus the market economy, individualism and collectivism, and the red world versus the free world. Both dominant ideologies were utopian.

In the Soviet Union, Marxism claimed to have discovered the laws of human existence, in which the conflict between capital and labour, between management and workers, was conceived of as a drama in which the actors play preordained roles which they are powerless to change. The dénouement, revolution, is inevitable and therefore certain. Marxists inhabited the kingdom of certainty. This had great benefits but also great disadvantages. It provided a map of the world and the conviction that history was moving in the right direction. The Soviet Union would one day be the leading world power and America, which appeared to be so powerful and threatening, would become socialist. The downside was that once Marxism had been codified into a ruling ideology, it became inflexible. There was always a gap between the party line and reality. The Soviet leadership revealed no interest in critical Marxism, a Marxism which would be consistently revised to take into consideration changes in the world. Only Gorbachev was capable of escaping from orthodox Marxism but he acted too late. The command economy, regarded as the cornerstone of a communist society, failed to generate the economic growth to satisfy the population. This presaged economic collapse. Elements of the market could have been introduced, but this would have resulted in greater inequality in Russia and the ruling Party elite would not have exercised the influence it did. Russia's aim was a strong state and its leaders believed this could only be achieved through strong or big government. The country concentrated on the internal market and, hence, foreign trade was not considered important. Economic growth did not depend on the expansion of foreign trade. Hence, the Soviet Union did not need to learn much about the thought patterns and ways of foreigners. Knowing and understanding other nations is critically important to trading nations. Also, the latter are more acutely aware of changes in technology, culture and taste in the outside world.

America also had a utopian ideology. It was articulated by Woodrow Wilson and was born of the conviction that Americans had the right and duty to enlighten the world. America had discovered the laws of human existence and was willing to enlighten others. To become rich, happy and free other nations had just to copy the United States. This meant acknowledging American hegemony throughout the world. Other terms can be used – universalism, internationalism, the new world order – to describe this phenomenon.

It was almost inevitable that Russia and America, given their utopianism, would construct empires. The number of countries which were in the respective zone of imperial influence would be used as a bench mark to determine which was gaining the upper hand. This was the essence of zero sum diplomacy. By the 1970s, superpower rivalry, beginning in Europe in 1945, had encompassed the globe. The American outreach was called the pax americana, the American peace or peace brought about by America. The Soviet version was dubbed the pax sovietica, or Soviet peace. Both were mutually exclusive and neither regarded the other as legitimate.

The negative evaluation of the Soviet Union by the Americans emerged during the Stalin period. The image of Russia as expansionist, aggressive, totalitarian, consolidated in the late 1940s and remained until the late 1980s. Mutual respect and trust disappeared at the same time and only returned under Gorbachev. The Cold War also damaged the American political system. Presidents, believing that it was their duty to intervene world-wide and faced with a Congress and people who were very sceptical, circumvented the legislature and the law to achieve their ends. This applied especially to Johnson, Nixon, Reagan and Bush, who became as deceitful as any Russian ruler. Another tactic was to exaggerate the danger so as to frighten everyone into following the President. Truman was the master of this manoeuvre. In this way the concept of the communist threat took root in America.

A HARD LESSON FOR THE SUPERPOWERS: EMPIRES ARE LIABILITIES

The lesson of the 1990s was that empires are liabilities, not assets. The greatest European empires, measured in terms of the magnitude of the territory acquired in relation to the size of the mother country, were Portugal, Spain, France, the Netherlands, Great Britain and Russia. None appears to have gained lasting benefit from their vast territories overseas. The so-called glittering prizes of imperial power deflected attention from domestic concerns and distorted economic life. The United States followed in the footsteps of the European empires and paid a very heavy price for its lack of historical awareness. America, in 1945, was an anti-imperial power which desired to see the great European empires buried. By the 1980s, it was acting in the same manner as the nineteenth-century European imperialists.

The conflict in Britain at the turn of the century was between liberalism and imperialism. The former argued that the wealth, prosperity and well-being of a nation was not related to its political power. Smaller nations, exercising little political influence, were often the most prosperous. The imperialists countered that war and the extension of empire were the way of the world and therefore good. If Britain did not seize a territory, its competitor could do so and place London at a disadvantage. This is an earlier example of zero sum diplomacy. The liberals thought that free trade was of fundamental significance. Openness to trade enhances prosperity and makes it possible for small states to become richer, in per capita terms, than large states. The imperialists preferred imperial preference. A common market was created to promote trade among the various parts of the empire and tariffs were set to prevent outsiders competing effectively in the imperial market. This arrangement benefited the large British companies but penalised others. The rest of the empire would have been better off with free trade, allowing all suppliers to come into the market. Unfortunately for Britain and the world, the imperialists won the argument in 1914.

IS THERE A LINK BETWEEN GOOD GOVERNMENT AND ECONOMIC PROSPERITY?

There is also a correlation between countries enjoying good governance and sound policies and economic prosperity. In these, real income per capita grew by 3 per cent annually between 1964 and 1993. In countries where there was poor government but reasonable policies, annual growth was down to 1.4 per cent. In countries where there was neither good governance nor good policies, growth was 0.4 per cent annually. There is also a direct relationship between the size of a country and economic growth.

In 1997 ten countries have populations over 100 million. Only two, the US and Japan, are rich. The others, China, India, Indonesia, Brazil, Russia, Pakistan, Bangladesh and Nigeria, are remarkable for their modest per capita incomes and the difficulties their governments face in achieving control and ruling effectively. The US and Japan are exceptions to the rule that large states are not wealthy, and special reasons appear to apply. The rule is that a small state encounters less difficulty in achieving good government and sound economic policies. But the US and Japan are market economies and dedicated to expanding exports. All communist states faced enormous problems in achieving economic growth and neglected exports.

How does all this apply to the superpowers? Both became expanding empires and the lesson of history is that all empires are eventually a burden. Another lesson is that a state cannot develop economically without sound government and policies. The post-1945 era was special, it was the era of de-colonialisation. This meant that many new states came into existence without indigenous leaderships. Often, tribes or clans competed for power as the territory they inherited had not previously been ruled as an entity in pre-imperial days. Unfortunately, good government has to be learnt and takes time.

The United States came to accept authoritarian government in South Korea as a bulwark to communism. It did the same in southeast Asia where fighting the communists took precedence. In Vietnam, the United States deluded itself into thinking that the first priority was military victory. Good government could then follow. In Africa, in the 1970s, the US again gave priority to military victory as the prelude to a better life. In the Middle East, America concerned itself little with social problems. In Guatemala and El Salvador, Washington ignored the social context and concentrated on military force.

The Soviet Union fared no better. It was mindful of the social context but equated good government and sound policies with Party leadership and a planned economy. It helped the Vietnamese to power but did not control them. Castro was not willing to heed Moscow's advice on many occasions. In Angola and Ethiopia, the Russians and Cubans fought alongside their clients. Moscow and Washington were fighting a losing battle in Africa. Angola was too large and diverse, as was Congo (Zaire). Ethiopia itself was an empire. Afghanistan was too large and ethnically divided to permit Moscow's will to be done.

Both superpowers poured vast sums into their empires and most of it was wasted. Much of it was military and this fuelled conflict. One estimate of the number of military-related deaths in the Third World is 21.8 million. Another lesson of the 1990s is that only a market economy generates rising prosperity over decades. Expanding trade is needed as the internal market is soon exhausted.

It was asking too much of the Americans, although they were convinced of the accuracy of these maxims, to have taken a relaxed view of communist expansion. The greatest difficulty in moving to good government and policies promoting economic growth and trade is being encountered by those states, notably Russia and Vietnam, in which the military were or are strong. Resistance to expanding trade, which involves attracting foreign direct investment, is linked to retaining a traditional way of life. Interest groups in the US still resist free trade but the global economy is becoming a reality. China flirted with empire for a short period in the 1970s, especially in Angola and Tanzania, but quickly decided it was not worth the effort. The conflicts with Russia, India and Vietnam were not geared to acquiring influence but forcing neighbours to respect Beijing.

WAS THE GROWTH OF THE NUCLEAR ARSENALS INEVITABLE?

The imperative of security was fuelled by the perceptions of both sides that incremental growth in their nuclear arsenals served peace and was defensive. Neither superpower, until the late Gorbachev era, was willing to concede that each innovation was perceived by the other as a new and more ominous threat. Stalin was usually prudent and always drew back from directly challenging the United States. That could be done by others, for example North Korea. Truman and Eisenhower enjoyed nuclear superiority and were not adverse to using blackmail against the Russians and Chinese. Eisenhower, as a military man, knew that the supposed Russian superiority, of which Khrushchev was bragging, was a fiction. He even decided to allow the Soviets to be first in space. He was confident of America's power and restricted the military budget.

Kennedy was more confrontational and less secure about the US's superiority. Khrushchev pushed him to the limit in Berlin and Cuba. Neither wished to use nuclear weapons but there was always the risk that a conflict could have occurred. Just as the reasons for the outbreak of the First World War are not fully understood, so it was possible for nuclear war to occur by accident. Cuba was the last nuclear confrontation between the superpowers. It introduced realism and the desire to reach arms control agreements.

WHY DID THE COLD WAR END?

The Cold War came to an end because it was impossible for two powers to divide and rule the world. The willpower had drained away. The burden was so great that the Soviet Union buckled and then disintegrated. By 1991, the United States was no longer able to intervene at will and was immensely relieved when the need to do so, the communist threat, melted away. The vast resources poured into imperial wars and the arms race exacerbated tensions in American society. Kennedy and Johnson's great society remained a utopia.

The Cold War internationalised local conflicts, most tragically in Indo-China and Angola. Had it not been deemed necessary to support anti-communist rulers, it is unlikely the US would have bothered about the Third World. Americans had realised that trade was a more effective way to become rich than an expanding empire. The non-aligned movement, led by Yugoslavia, and consisting mainly of Third World states, was pro-Soviet. Moscow advertised itself as anti-imperialist, anti-colonialist and the friend of the Third World. Afghanistan ruined all that. Countries like India developed close ties with Russia. Fabian socialism and the desire to regulate almost everything inclined India to follow Russia. In 1949, per capita income in India and China was about the same. In 1997, China's was about double that of India. Delhi's policies have not served its people well.

AMERICA'S CHANGING DOCTRINE

America's response to regional conflicts changed over time. Beginning with Korea, it was willing to send its own troops to fight in wars in foreign fields. Many presidents gave their names to doctrines:

- the Truman doctrine, which protected Greece, Turkey and, indirectly, other states;

- the Eisenhower doctrine, which identified the Middle East as of great strategic importance to the US;

- the Nixon doctrine, which envisaged the building up of regional allies to resist communist subversion; America would supply the technology but the locals would do the fighting;

- the Carter doctrine, in the wake of the Soviet invasion of Afghanistan, envisaged America intervening with its own troops if the Persian Gulf region were threatened;

- the end of the Cold War meant that Bush, in countering Iraqi aggression, in 1990, did not give his name to a new doctrine. He merely referred to Iraq as an 'outside force'. He could engage militarily in Kuwait with the blessing of the UN Security Council, for the first time since 1950. Instead of a doctrine, he proclaimed the new world order, with the UN playing the role originally intended for it.

The present level of prosperity in the world is inconceivable without the Bretton Woods agreement. It established the US dollar as the world's trading currency. The generosity of the Americans kick-started west European economic recovery (although there is a revisionist view which claims it was not really necessary). The willingness of Washington to open its doors to imports led to western Europe and Japan flourishing. This then encompassed Hong Kong, South Korea, Taiwan, Indonesia, Malaysia, Singapore and Thailand. Another factor was the US willingness to export high technology to friendly states. The GDP of EU states, in the mid-1990s, was higher than that of the US.

It is striking that of the countries which benefited most, the US only intervened militarily and fought a war in South Korea. Without the Cold War, America almost certainly would not have been so generous. The best defence against the spread of communist influence was affluence. GATT played an important role in expanding trade and was followed by the more ambitious World Trade Agreement (WTA). On the other hand, some of the countries where the US intervened were, and have remained, the poorest in the world: Angola, Congo (Zaire), Somalia, Vietnam, Cambodia, Laos, Guatemala and El Salvador.

WAS THE US AN IMPERIALIST POWER?

The US was an imperialist power after 1944, but it was benign imperialism. The world is now richer and more secure because of it. Had it not been for the arms race, the Soviet Union might still be a communist state. It had to devote about two-thirds of its scientists and about a third of its economy to its military effort. Whereas there was a spin-off in the US from military research and development, there was almost none in Russia.

The end of the Cold War has resulted in greater disarray in Russia than in the United States. It is still searching for its role in the world. China has benefited greatly. Its most difficult task is to manage political change, which is inevitable given the rapid economic growth. Wars, now, are rarely between states, and never between developed states, but within countries. Marxism is very rarely an issue nowadays. Nationalism and ethnic or clan loyalties are much more likely to be the genesis of conflict. The world was relatively simple to understand during the Cold War. It is now extremely complex. The threat of a nuclear holocaust is no longer real. Wars have reverted to being conventional. The greatest threat to life on this planet is no longer war but the destruction of the environment. There are now two camps, those who pollute most, led again by the US, and the rest. The world is always divided [1, 9, 17, 22, 37, 41, 48, 53, 57].

PART FOUR: DOCUMENTS

DOCUMENT 1 KHRUSHCHEV AND DIVERSIONARY
TACTICS

*Khrushchev, four days before he was elected Party leader, in September
1953, signed this order to the Ministry of Internal Affairs (MVD), making
the ministry responsible for certain espionage and other activities.*

Central Committee, Communist Party of the Soviet Union   Secret Confidential
Special Dossier

Resolution

On the organisation of the 12th section (special) in the 2nd principal
directorate (espionage), USSR

MVD
Moscow

1) The USSR Minister of the Interior [Kruglov] is to organise in the 2nd
principal directorate of the MVD (espionage) a 12th section (special) to
engage in diversionary operations against important strategic military
targets and communications routes in the leading aggressor states, the
United States and Great Britain, and also in other capitalist states being
used as the main aggressors against the USSR.

Terror attacks [crossed out and corrected by hand, 'active operations'] are
justified against the most active and the most bitter enemies of the Soviet
Union in capitalist states, the most dangerous foreign spies, the leaders of
anti-Soviet émigré organisations and traitors.

2) Arrange for all enterprises [gulag] of the USSR MVD under section 12 to
be inspected and approved by the Presidium [Politburo] of the CC, CPSU.

3) Register the statute, the structure and the personnel of the 12th section
(special) of the 2nd principal directorate (espionage) of the USSR MVD.

Secretary of the CC, CPSU
N. Khrushchev

Boukovsky [7], pp. 114–15.

DOCUMENT 2   KHRUSHCHEV AND CHINA

(a) Mao felt insulted when he visited Moscow for the first time, in 1950, as head of the People's Republic of China. He asked for substantial aid but was only given a modest loan, on which he was required to pay interest. When Stalin died Mao regarded himself as the doyen of world communist leaders and expected to be consulted on all major issues. However, Khrushchev had no intention of treating Mao in this fashion, in 1957, and wanted to demonstrate that the Soviet Union was dominant, but found Mao unfathomable.

'If there is an attack on the Soviet Union, I would recommend that you do not offer resistance.'

I was immediately on my guard. The imperialist states attack the Soviet union, and we must not offer resistance? How could this be? What were we supposed to do?

Mao Zedong explained: 'Retreat for a year, or two or three. Force your enemy to stretch out his lines of communications. That will weaken him. Then, with our combined strength, we will go for the enemy together and smash him.'

I said: 'Comrade Mao, I don't know what to say. What you are saying is out of the question. Can you imagine us retreating for a year? Would the war go on for a year? Think about what can happen in a year!'

Mao answered: 'But in World War II you retreated to Stalingrad for two years. Why can't you retreat for three years now? If you retreat to the Urals, China is nearby. We'll use our resources and territory to smash the enemy.'

I said: 'Comrade Mao, we see things differently. We believe in immediate retaliation, with all the weapons at our disposal. Our ability to do that is what deters our enemy. We can keep him from committing aggression in the first place.'

'No,' said Mao, 'I don't think that's right.'

Later, I often wondered how to argue against such reasoning. Mao is a clever man. How could he think this way? Could it have been a provocation? I can't believe Mao would try something so stupid with us. Could he really have believed that what he was saying made military sense?

Khrushchev [42], pp. 147–50.

(b) This extract is by Shmuel Mikunis, then leader of the Israeli Communist Party. It captures nicely Mao's vanity.

In the way he spoke and held himself, and in the way he replied to questions, [Mao Zedong] resembled a sage of ancient China. He gave me the impression, at any rate, when I saw him for the first time in St George's Hall [in the Kremlin]. He had trouble with his legs and usually spoke sitting down. His favourite theme, to which he kept returning, was World War III. He regarded it as an absolutely inevitable event, for which one must be ready at any moment. I would even go so far as to say he lived and thought in terms of this war, as though it had already begun. I well remember how he sat there, surrounded by Soviet delegates, and philosophised aloud: 'Nehru and I', he said, 'are at present discussing the question of how many people would perish in an atomic war. Nehru says we'll lose a billion and a half, but I say only a billion and a quarter'.

Palmiro Togliatti then asked him: 'But what would become of Italy as a result of such a war?' Mao Zedong looked at him in a thoughtful way and replied, quite coolly: 'But who told you that Italy must survive? Three hundred million Chinese will be left, and that will be enough for the human race to continue' ... He talked a lot, but in an absolutely peremptory way: he did not really talk but insist.

Vremya i My (Tel Aviv), no. 48, 1979, pp. 164–5.

DOCUMENT 3   KENNEDY AND VIETNAM

In January 1961, ten days before his inauguration, President-elect Kennedy, at his request, met the evangelist Billy Graham for a game of golf in Florida. Among the things they discussed was foreign policy. Here, Kennedy reveals that he was an adherent of the domino theory, if one country falls to the communists then its neighbours will as well. He already has firm ideas about Vietnam.

In the clubhouse afterward, we got into a lively discussion. Kennedy aired his view that the sixties would be filled with challenges, promises, and problems. As we sat relaxing with soft drinks, he began to talk about Vietnam. Kennedy agreed with Eisenhower's domino theory. 'If Laos goes', he said, 'all of Southeast Asia will go. Then India. We're going to have to do something about it. Eisenhower's got a number of people over there. We can't allow Vietnam to fall to the Communists.'

' That was the first time I heard that Vietnam – that far-off country in the Orient – was such a problem. It all sounded so remote to me.

Graham [26], p. 395.

DOCUMENT 4   KENNEDY, KHRUSHCHEV AND CUBA

(a) President John F. Kennedy wanted to improve relations with the Soviet Union, but in this extract from a conversation in July 1959 he reveals his pessimism. However, he is prescient about the desire of Soviet-dominated countries, especially in eastern Europe, and also non-Russian nationalities in the Soviet Union, to be free.

You have to first decide what is the motive force of the Soviet Union. Is it merely to provide security for them, and in order to provide security for the Russian mainland, do they have to have friendly countries on the borders? ... Or is it evangelical, that communists can, by continuing to press on us, weaken us so that eventually they can [achieve] world revolution?

I guess, probably, obviously, a combination of the two. So therefore, I don't think there is any button that you press that reaches an accommodation with the Soviet Union which is hard and fast ... What it is is a constant day to day struggle with an enemy who is constantly attempting to expand his power ... You have two people, neither of whom – who are both of good will, but neither of whom can communicate because of a language difference ...

I don't think there's any magic solution to solve or really ease East–West [tension] at the present time. Now maybe a successor to Khrushchev – or even Khrushchev himself ... It's like those ads you see in the *Sunday* [*New York*] *Times* ... about some fellow in a beard about 'he releases the magic power within you' ... The magic power really is the desire of everyone to be independent and every nation to be independent. That's the basic force which is really, I think, the strong force on our side. That's the magic power, and that's what's going to screw the Russians ultimately.

Beschloss [3], p. 20.

(b) On Wednesday 24 October 1962, during the Cuban missile crisis, President Kennedy received the rudest letter from a Soviet leader to an American President since the days of Stalin. The Americans had just imposed a quarantine around Cuba to prevent any more nuclear missiles or warheads being delivered.

Imagine, Mr. President, that we had presented you with the conditions of ultimatum that you have presented us by your action. How would you have reacted to this? ... Who asked you to do this? You, Mr. President are not declaring quarantines but advancing an ultimatum and threatening that unless we subordinate ourselves to your demands, you will use force.

Consider what you are saying! ... You are no longer appealing to reason, but wish to intimidate us ... And all this not only out of hatred for the Cuban people and their government, but also because of considerations having to do with the election campaign in the USA ... The actions of the

USA toward Cuba are outright banditry or, if you like, the folly of degenerate imperialism.

Unfortunately such folly can bring grave suffering to the peoples of all countries, not least the American people, since with the advent of modern types of armament, the USA has fully lost its invulnerability ... If someone had tried to dictate these kinds of conditions to you, you would have rejected them. And we also say – no ... We shall not be simply observers of the pirate-like actions of American ships on the high seas. We will be forced to take measures which we deem necessary and adequate to protect our rights.

Beschloss [3], p. 501.

(c) On Friday 26 October 1962, President Kennedy received a letter from Khrushchev. It contained corrections of the original text by Khrushchev himself. It had clearly been put together in a hurry and had not been sent from the Kremlin to the Ministry of Foreign Affairs for the official seal to be attached. Khrushchev's assurance that Soviet ships, en route to Cuba, were not carrying weapons was false. They were transporting nuclear war heads.

In the name of the Soviet government and the Soviet people, I assure you that your conclusions regarding offensive weapons in Cuba are groundless ... You are a military man and, I hope, will understand me ...

You are mistaken if you think that any of our weapons on Cuba are offensive. However, let us not quarrel now. It is apparent that I will not be able to convince you of this. But I say to you – you, Mr. President, are a military man and should understand – can one attack if one has on one's territory even an enormous quantity of missiles of various effective radiuses and various power, but using only these means. These missiles are a means of extermination and destruction. But one cannot attack with these missiles – even nuclear missiles of a power of a hundred megatonnes, because only people, troops, can attack. Without people, any weapons, however powerful, cannot be offensive.

Therefore how can one give such a completely incorrect interpretation as you are now giving, to the effect that some sort of weapons on Cuba are offensive? All the weapons located there, and I assure you of this, have a defensive character, are on Cuba solely for the purpose of defence, and we have sent them to Cuba at the request of the Cuban government. You, however, say that these are offensive weapons.

Mr. President, do you seriously think that Cuba can attack the United States and that even we together with Cuba can attack you from Cuban territory? ... I assure you that on those ships, which are bound for Cuba, there are no weapons at all. The weapons necessary for the defence of Cuba are already there ... I propose: we, for our part, will declare that our ships bound for Cuba will not carry any kind of armaments. You will declare that the United States will not invade Cuba with its forces and will not support any kind of forces that might intend to carry out an invasion of Cuba. Then the necessity for the presence of our military specialists in Cuba will disappear.

Beschloss [3], pp. 517–20.

(d) On Sunday 28 October 1962, Radio Moscow broadcast the tenth message between Khrushchev and Kennedy.

I very well understand your anxiety and that of the American people about the fact that the weapons you describe as offensive are formidable weapons indeed ...

In order to eliminate as rapidly as possible the conflict which endangers the cause of peace ... the Soviet government, in addition to previously issued instructions to cease further work on weapons construction sites, has issued a new order to dismantle the weapons which you describe as offensive, and to crate and return them to the Soviet Union ...

Mr. President ... I respect and trust the statement you have made in your message ... that there would be no attack or invasion against Cuba, not only by the United States but other countries of the Western Hemisphere ... Therefore the motives which induced us to give aid of this kind to Cuba have disappeared ...

We are prepared to reach an agreement to enable United Nations representatives to verify the dismantling of these weapons.

Beschloss [3], p. 541.

DOCUMENT 5   KISSINGER, BREZHNEV AND DÉTENTE

(a) Henry Kissinger visited the Soviet Union in early May 1973 to prepare the ground for a summit between Brezhnev and Nixon. He gives a caustic account of Brezhnev and his milieu.

The American party was housed in an East German-built villa resembling an oversized Swiss chalet blown out of scale by the heavy stolidity that in the Communist world denotes status. The exterior looked vaguely Alpine; the inside was all velvet-covered Victorian opulence.

The largest private residence in the compound belonged to Brezhnev. It was a two-storey chalet built in the same style as my residence, though on an even grander scale ...

Brezhnev came to my residence soon after my arrival and greeted me boisterously. A little later he invited my colleagues and me to dinner at his villa, which he first showed off with all the pride of a self-made entrepreneur. He asked me how much such an establishment would cost in the United States. I guessed tactlessly and mistakenly at four hundred thousand dollars. Brezhnev's face fell. My associate, Helmut Sonnenfeldt, was psychologically more adept: two million, he corrected – probably much closer to the truth. Brezhnev, vastly reassured, beamed and resumed his private tour ...

Brezhnev conducted almost all the negotiations for the Soviets; only highly technical subjects, such as the European Security Conference, were left to Foreign Minister Andrei Gromyko. Brezhnev's repertory of jokes seemed as inexhaustible as the previous year's, now spiced with a new familiarity that probably went further than he intended. His drinking was less restrained ...

The timetable was, as usual, enigmatic. No schedule or advance indication of subjects was ever given, even though Brezhnev had no other visible program ... Twice, when our conversation did not come up to Brezhnev's hopes – on the Middle East, and on some dispute over the nuclear agreement – he sulked in his villa and refused to schedule another session. ... When I maintained my position – simply by putting forward no additional thoughts – Brezhnev suddenly materialized again as if nothing had happened. His ploy having failed, he would then do the best with what he had and set about to restore an atmosphere of ebullient goodwill ...

Brezhnev could not hear often enough my avowal that we were proceeding on the premise of equality – an attitude inconceivable in Peking, whose leaders thought of themselves as culturally superior whatever the statistics showed about relative material strength. Brezhnev endlessly sought reassurance that he would be courteously received in America, that he would not be exposed to hostile demonstrations, and that he would have the chance to meet 'ordinary' people ...

One day he called for me in the black Cadillac sedan that Dobrynin had suggested might be a suitable state gift for Nixon to bring the year before ... With Brezhnev at the wheel, we took off along winding country roads at speeds that made one pray hopelessly for some policeman's intervention, unlikely as it was that a traffic cop – if indeed they existed in the countryside – would dare halt the General Secretary. Thus propelled to a boat landing, Brezhnev bundled me off onto a hydrofoil – mercifully not driven by him – which nevertheless seemed determined to break the speed record established by the General Secretary in getting me there. My brain being addled by these multiple jolts, I lack a precise recollection of this excursion. ...

One afternoon I returned to my villa and found hunting attire ... It was an elegant, military-looking olive drab, with high boots, for which I am unlikely to have any further use. Brezhnev, similarly attired, collected me in a jeep driven, I was grateful to notice, by a game warden. Since I hate the killing of animals for sport, I told Brezhnev that I would come along in my capacity as adviser. He said some wild boars had already been earmarked for me. Given my marksmanship, I replied, the cause of death would have to be heart failure ...

All was absolutely still. Only Brezhnev's voice could be heard, whispering tales of hunting adventures: of his courage when a boar had once attacked his jeep; of the bison that stuffed itself with the grain and potatoes laid out as bait and then fell contentedly asleep on the steps of the hunting tower, trapping Soviet Defense Minister Marshal Rodion Malinovski in the tower until a search party rescued him ...

Kissinger [46], pp. 229–32.

(b) Brezhnev took the Chinese threat very seriously and here warns the United States against aiding China militarily.

Brezhnev's split personality – alternatively boastful and insecure, belligerent and mellow – was in plain view ... The truculence appeared in his discussion of China. He began describing the experiences of his brother who had worked there as an engineer before Khrushchev removed all Soviet advisers. He had found the Chinese treacherous, arrogant, beyond the human pale. They were cannibalistic in the way they destroyed their top leaders (an amazing comment from a man who had launched his career during Stalin's purges); they might well, in fact, be cannibals. Now China was acquiring a nuclear arsenal. The Soviet Union could not accept this passively; something would have to be done. He did not say what.

Brezhnev was clearly fishing for some hint of American acquiescence in a Soviet preemptive attack. I gave no encouragement; my bland response was that the growth of China was one of those problems that underlined the importance of settling disputes peacefully. Brezhnev contemptuously ignored this high-minded theory and returned to his preoccupation. China's growing military might was a threat to everybody. Any military assistance to it by the United States would lead to war ... the next day Dobrynin took me aside to stress that the China portion of the discussion in the hunting blind was not to be treated as social. Brezhnev had meant every word of it.

Kissinger [46], p. 233.

(c) Here Henry Kissinger defends his policy of détente and ruminates on the loss of American hegemony.

Détente did not prevent resistance to Soviet expansion: on the contrary, it fostered the only psychologically possible framework for such resistance. [President] Nixon knew where to draw the line against Soviet adventure whether it occurred directly or through proxy, as in Cienfuegos, Jordan, along the Suez Canal, and during the Indian-Pakistan war ... If the Vietnam war had taught us anything, it was that a military confrontation could be sustained only if the American people were convinced there was no other choice ...

The United States and the Soviet Union are ideological rivals. Détente cannot change that. The nuclear age compels us to coexist. Rhetorical crusades cannot change that, either.

Our age must learn the lessons of World War II, brought about when the democracies failed to understand the designs of a totalitarian aggressor, sought foolishly to appease him, and permitted him to achieve a military superiority. This must never happen again ...

An American President thus has a dual responsibility: He must resist Soviet expansionism. And he must be conscious of the profound risks of global confrontation. His policy must embrace both deterrence and coexistence, both containment and an effort to relax tensions ... Yet if we pursue the ideological conflict divorced from strategy, if confrontation turns into an end in itself, we will lose the cohesion of our alliances and ultimately the confidence of our people. That was what the Nixon Administration understood by détente ...

The late 1960s had marked the end of the period of American predominance based on overwhelming nuclear and economic supremacy. The Soviet nuclear stockpile was inevitably approaching parity. The economic strength of Japan and Europe was bound to lead them to seek larger political influence. The new, developing nations pressed their claims to greater power and participation. The United States would have to learn to base its foreign policy on premises analogous to those by which other nations historically had conducted theirs. The percentage of the world's Gross National Product represented by our economy was sinking by 10 per cent with every decade: from 52 per cent in 1950 to 40 per cent in 1960, to some 30 per cent in 1970 (and 22 per cent now – 1982) ... Still the strongest nation but no longer preeminent, we would have to take seriously the world balance of power, for if it tilted against us, it might prove irreversible ...

The strategy of the Nixon Administration presupposed a decisive President willing to stake American power to resist Soviet expansionism and ready to negotiate seriously if the Soviets would accept coexistence on this basis. But both of these courses of action were being destroyed by our domestic passion play ... I am convinced, for a long range policy that avoids either confrontation for its own sake or acquiescence in Soviet expansion, we must resist marginal accretions of Soviet power even when the issues seem ambiguous.

Kissinger [46], pp. 237–8.

(d) Kissinger explains the reasons for the failure of his foreign policy.

Still, I reflect with melancholy on the way America consumed its unity in 1973–1974 ...

There is no question in my mind that one of the casualties of the period was a balanced, careful, thoughtful approach to East–West relations. The sober teaching of the 1973–1974 period is that idealism did not, in the end, enhance the human rights of Jews in the Soviet Union (the emigration figure for 1975 was less than 40 per cent of that of 1973); that the undermining of SALT did not improve our military posture ... The approach being legislated did not deter Soviet expansion. That increased, and the same domestic divisions that had spawned the confrontation prevented an effective response. The Soviet Union was not induced to behave in a more reasonable manner. The Administration had no illusions about Soviet purposes, but the domestic debate confused, instead of illuminated, the nation's understanding of the complexity of our challenge.

Kissinger [46], p. 1030.

DOCUMENT 6   THE KGB

These Party documents reveal the wide-ranging activities of the Soviet authorities in their never-ending struggle to undermine American power in the United States and Central America.

(a)

KGB,	Secret Confidential
USSR Council of Ministers,	Special Dossier
28 April 1970	
No. 1128–A	
Moscow	
CPSU Central Committee	

Lately, the radical black organisation, the Black Panthers, has been subjected to ferocious repression by the US authorities, under the command of the FBI, which regards the Black Panthers as a serious threat to national security.

As the Black Panthers is an organisation representing blacks, dynamic and dangerous for the ruling classes of the United States, the Communist Party [of the USA] is attempting to influence it, in a positive manner. This policy of the communist party is beginning to bear fruit.

Since the growth of the Negro protest movement will create difficulties for the ruling circles of the United States, and will lead the Nixon administration to develop an active foreign policy, we think it advisable to implement a series of measures to strengthen and enlarge this organisation. Hence we propose, based on the capabilities of the KGB in the countries of Africa, to encourage politicians and popular figures, youth organisations, trade unions and nationalist groups to forward petitions, statements and declarations, supporting the rights of Negroes in America, to the UN, to representatives of the US in those countries and to the government of the United States. Publish in the press of several African states articles and letters accusing the American government of genocide. Make use of the facilities of the KGB in New York and Washington to influence the Black Panthers to forward to the UN and other organisations petitions requesting their help to end the policy of genocide being conducted by American authorities against American Negroes.

It is correct to assume that, after the above measures have been set in motion, it will be possible to mobilise public opinion in the United States and in third countries to support American Negroes and also to encourage the Black Panthers to step up their campaign.

Chair of the KGB
Andropov

Boukovsky [7], pp. 35–6.

(b)
To be returned within three days to the Central Committee, CPSU Secret Confidential
(general service, 2nd section)   Special Dossier
No. St–37 gs
27 December 1976

Extract from the minutes no. 37, para. 37 gs, CC Secretariat

For the attention of the international department, CC, CPSU

Responding to the request of the leadership of the Communist Party of Argentina, the Popular Party of Panama, the Communist Party of El Salvador and the Communist Party of Uruguay, welcome to the USSR *for training in the techniques of Party security, espionage and counter-espionage, 10 Argentinian communists, three Panamanians, three Salvadorans, three Uruguayans, for a period of six months.*

The organisation of their training is to be the responsibility of the KGB, USSR Council of Ministers; welcome, services and assistance will be the duty of the international department and the administration of affairs of the CC, CPSU. The travel expenses of the 10 Argentinian comrades from Buenos to Moscow and return, of the three Panamanians from Panama to Moscow and return, of the three Salvadorans from San Salvador to Moscow and return, and the three Uruguayans from Montevideo to Moscow and return will be charged to the Party budget.

Secretary of the CC

For: comrades Andropov, Ponomarev, Pavlov

Boukovsky [7], p. 37.

(c)

No. St–224/71 gs   Secret Confidential
18 August 1980   Special Dossier

Resolution of the CC Secretariat, CPSU

For the attention of the international department, CC, CPSU

Responding to the request of the leadership of the Communist Party of El
Salvador, admit, in 1980, thirty Salvadoran communists, already in the
USSR, *for military training for a period of six months.* Welcome, services,
material assistance, *organisation of the training* of the thirty Salvadoran
communists, as well as their travel expenses from Moscow to Salvador will
be *charged to the budget of the Ministry of Defence.*

[Signed: A. Chernyaev]

Those who voted: (signatures) Kirilenko, Zimyanin, Gorbachev, Kapitonov,
Dolgikh

Copies to: comrades Ustinov, Ponomarev
Distributed on 18 August 1980

Boukovsky [7], p. 38.

(d)

                                                    Secret Confidential
                                                    (Translated from Spanish)

To the CC, CPSU

Dear comrades,

I request you to welcome thirty members of our young communists living in
Moscow *for military training* for four or five months in the following
branches:
1) six comrades in *military espionage*
2) eight comrades to be specially trained as *commanders of guerrilla
detachments*
3) five comrades as *artillery commanders*
4) five comrades as *diversionary tactics commanders*
5) six comrades in *communications*

I thank you for the help the CPSU has extended our Party.

Shafik Handal

General secretary of the CC, Communist Party of El Salvador
23 July 1980, Moscow
Translation: V. Tikhmenev

Boukovsky [7], p. 38.

(e)

No. St–225/5 gs   Secret Confidential
20 August 1980   Special Dossier

Resolution of the CC Secretariat, CPSU

For the attention of the leadership of the Communist Party of El Salvador

1) Responding to the request of the leadership of the Communist Party of
   El Salvador, the Ministry of Civil Transport Aviation, during
   September–October of this year, is to transport *fire arms and western
   produced munitions,* weighing 60 to 80 tonnes, from Hanoi [Vietnam]
   to Havana [Cuba], to be forwarded by our Cuban comrades to our
   friends in Salvador.
   The costs of transporting the *arms* from Hanoi to Havana will be
   charged to the state aid budget and not any foreign state.
2) The texts of the telegrams to the Soviet ambassadors to Cuba and
   Vietnam (enclosed) are confirmed.

[Signed: Chernyaev]

Those who voted: Kirilenko, Russakov, Gorbachev, Dolgikh, Zimyanin,
Kapitonov
Copies to: comrades Gromyko, Ponomarev
to comrades: Bugaev, Garbuzov (without the enclosed)

Boukovsky [7], p. 39.

(f)

Havana   Secret Confidential
                                             Special Dossier
                          Addendum no. 1 of the PV 5 gs pr. 225
                                             Urgent
                    To the Soviet Ambassador

662. *Inform Shafik Handal, general secretary of the CC, Communist Party
of El Salvador, or, if he is absent, a member of the leadership of the
Communist Party of El Salvador, that his request for the transport of
western manufactured arms from Vietnam to Cuba has been considered by
our authorities and is granted.* Inform our Cuban friends also and add that

we have taken this decision in the light of the provisional agreement which has already been reached by comrades F. Castro and S. Handal.

For your information: the delivery of the *arms* will be by Aeroflot planes. Ensure the indispensable cooperation necessary for the organisation of these deliveries to our Cuban friends in Havana for onward transfer to our Salvadoran friends.

Report on the implementation of the above.

[Signed: Chernyaev, Russakov]

Boukovsky [7], pp. 39–40.

DOCUMENT 7   **THE KGB AND ITALY**

In 1974 the Italian Communist Party became concerned about a lurch to the right in Italy and began to fear for the safety of members. The following document is the CPSU's response to a request by the Italian communists for documents which would allow 50 comrades to cross France, in wigs and false beards, carrying French passports supplied by the KGB!

Proletarians of the World Unite!

To be returned within 24 hours to the CC, CPSU (general service, 2nd section)

Secret Confidential

Communist Party of the Soviet Union: Central Committee   Secret Dossier

P136/53

5 May 1974

To comrades Andropov, Ponomarev complete; paragraph 2 to Pavlov

Special assistance to the Italian Communist Party

1) Meet the request of the leadership of the Italian Communist Party (PCI) and welcome to the Soviet Union, for special training, nineteen Italian communists of which six are to study radio transmissions, work on the BR–3Y broadcasting stations and codes (for three months), two instructors for training radio telegraphers and encoders (three months), nine on Party techniques (two months), two for *altering the external appearance* (two weeks) and one specialist for discussions on the organisation of particular types of internal radio broadcasting (one week).

Meet the request of the leadership of the PCI and provide 500 blank and

50 completed (reserved for personnel and cadres of the PCI) Italian documents, for internal and external use, and 50 complete sets of documents of this type, French and Swiss, as well as wigs and the equipment for altering one's *external appearance*. The manufacture of the identity documents and the equipment for altering one's *external appearance* will be the responsibility of the international department of the CC, CPSU and the KGB, USSR Council of Ministers ...

The text of the telegram to the KGB *rezident* (head) in Italy is approved.

CC Secretary

Boukovsky [7], pp. 42–3.

DOCUMENT 8   THE RUSSIANS AND THE PALESTINIANS

The KGB supplied weapons on a regular basis to the Palestinians.

USSR KGB,	Very Important
USSR Council of Ministers	Special Dossier
16 May 1975	
No. 1218–A/ov	
Moscow	

To comrade L. I. Brezhnev

Following the decision of the CC, CPSU, the KGB delivered to Uadia Haddad, the person agreed by the KGB espionage services and the chief of the department for foreign affairs of the National Front for the Liberation of Palestine, a consignment of foreign manufactured arms and the necessary equipment (53 machine guns, 50 pistols of which 10 had silencers), 34,000 cartridges and bullets.

This delivery of these arms, which was illegal, was carried out in neutral waters in the gulf of Aden, at night, with as little contact as possible, in extreme secrecy, using a patrol vessel of the USSR Navy.

Haddad is the only foreigner aware that the above mentioned arms were delivered by us.

Chair of the KGB
Andropov

Boukovsky [7], p. 46.

DOCUMENT 9   AFGHANISTAN

(a) The Soviet decision to intervene in Afghanistan was taken by the Politburo on 12 December 1979, with the following present: Leonid Brezhnev, Party General Secretary; Yury Andropov, chair of the KGB; Dmitry Ustinov, Minister of Defence; Konstantin Chernenko; Arvid Pelshe; Mikhail Suslov; Andrei Kirilenko; Viktor Grishin; Nikolai Tikhonov. Boris Ponomarev was also present, but as a candidate member did not have the right to vote. Those who were absent but who signed the document later were: Dinmukhamed Kunaev, who signed on 25 December, and Grigory Romanov and Vladimir Shcherbitsky, on 26 December. The document itself, in Chernenko's handwriting, does not reveal the significance of the decision.

On the Situation in Afghanistan
1) Approve the views and measures outlined by comrades Andropov, Ustinov, Gromyko.
Changes may be made during the implementation of these measures but they may not undermine the principles laid down.
Submit in due course to the Politburo those decisions which require the approval of the Central Committee.
Comrades Andropov, Ustinov and Gromyko are responsible for implementing all these measures.
2) Comrades Andropov, Ustinov, Gromyko are to keep the Politburo informed about the implementation of the above measures.

L. Brezhnev
Secretary of the Central Committee
P176/125, 12 December 1979

Boukovsky [7], p. 383.

(b) A battalion of Spetsnaz (special forces), consisting of Central Asians, but commanded by a Russian, Lieutenant Colonel Kolesnik, had been forming since May 1979. The battalion, consisting of 500 men, was flown to Bahram, Afghanistan, in Afghan uniforms, and moved to Kabul, on 21 December. Two KGB units joined them. On 25 December, at 1500 hours Moscow time, Soviet troops crossed the border into Afghanistan. Most troops came by air. There were 343 flights spread over 47 hours, involving 7,700 men, 894 pieces of military equipment and 1,062 tonnes of supplies.

The immediate target for the KGB units was the palace in Kabul where Hafizullah Amin, the Afghan communist leader, was hiding (he thought the Russians were coming to save him). Amin and his personal guard (100 to 150 men) were to be killed and no survivors left alive.

On 27 December 1979 the Politburo informed foreign communist and workers' parties that the intervention in Afghanistan was 'provisional' and 'limited'. It provided more information, but only to its own officials throughout the Soviet Union: Afghanistan was of great strategic importance to Russian security, China was dangerously near, the capitalists would make a lot of the intervention, and then instructions were issued. (Boukovsky [7], p. 384.)

Any insinuation that there we have interfered in the internal affairs of Afghanistan is to be resolutely rebutted ... When commenting on the domestic changes which have occurred in Afghanistan, underline firmly that these are the domestic concerns of the Afghan people and support this with reference to the public statements of the Revolutionary Council and the speeches of the chair of the Revolutionary Council of Afghanistan, Babrak Karmal [appointed by Moscow to succeed Amin].

(c) The Soviet leadership did not grasp the catastrophe which had befallen them. They thought the west would protest, make some noise and then forget about the whole episode. They also did not grasp the damage they were doing to their relations with the Muslim world. At a Party Central Committee plenum, on 23 June 1980, Gromyko spoke eloquently of the growing power of the Soviet Union.

It is not possible to perceive correctly this or that tendency if one does not give due consideration to the most important factor in international affairs, the constant strengthening of the position of socialism on the international stage.
The world map bears eloquent testimony to this.
In the western hemisphere, there is glorious Cuba.
In south-east Asia, Vietnam is building a new life.
The large family of fraternal parties has welcomed Laos and the People's Republic of Kampuchea.
A form of socialist development is evident in different countries, in various continents: Angola, Ethiopia, South Yemen, and a short time ago, Afghanistan. We can also recall the example of Nicaragua and certain countries which have turned towards socialism ...
Despite the apparent solidarity of the NATO countries, class contradictions cannot fail to emerge. The United States embargo is not supported unanimously and many countries are dragging their feet: France, West Germany, Italy ...
Even England, which, despite the blow which has befallen it, in the person of Mrs. Thatcher, does not agree with Washington on everything. (Laughter in the hall)

The plenum approved the 'various types of aid' *extended to Afghanistan to prevent* 'attacks and interventions', *the aim of which was to* 'suffocate the Afghan revolution and to transform Afghanistan into a base of military aggression on the southern frontiers of the Soviet Union'. *It also called on the Politburo to* 'strengthen the fraternal union of the socialist states, peaceful co-existence, support the just struggle of peoples for their freedom and independence, the slowing down of the arms race, the maintenance and development of international détente, mutual economic, scientific and cultural cooperation ...'

Boukovsky [7], pp. 391–2.

DOCUMENT 10 POLAND

(a) Poland was an important country from Russia's point of view. Strategically, lines of communication to East Germany ran through Poland. Khrushchev, in 1956, was alarmed by events, and he and other members of the Soviet leadership visited Poland. He took it for granted that Russia had the right to ensure that Poland stayed in the socialist camp. A Politburo meeting on 22 January 1981 discussed the situation and how to cope with Solidarity, the trade union movement.

Brezhnev: We are all very alarmed by the recent turn of events in Poland. The worst thing is that our friends listen to us, agree with our recommendations but do nothing. Counter-revolution has been progressing on all fronts recently. Kania [Party leader] informed me on the telephone that the leadership had been criticised at the plenum. I replied that that was alright. 'It is not enough just to criticise you, but to wave the rubber truncheon. This would have made you understand.' These are literally my words. Comrade Kania has recognised that he has been acting too softly, that he has to be much harder. I told him: 'How often have we tried to explain to you that you have to take more energetic measures, that you cannot keep on making concessions to Solidarity? You only talk about the "peaceful way" without understanding or wanting to understand that the peaceful way which you are adopting can cost you blood' ... Perhaps we should send Andropov and Ustinov to Brest [on Belorussian-Polish border] to talk with comrades Kania and Jaruzelski.

Andropov: Leonid Ilich's [Brezhnev] proposals are absolutely correct. We have to increase our influence, our pressure on our friends.

Gromyko: Of course, American and east European information on the Polish situation is presented in a tendentious way. It spells out the 'justification' for the demands of Solidarity and the anti-social forces in Poland and the inability of the Polish leadership to cope with the domestic situation. We are being advised not to intervene militarily in the internal situation in Poland.

I have to inform you that the state of mind of Kania and Jaruzelski is not encouraging. Certain hints point to the fact that Jaruzelski is beaten and does not know what to do ... The Poles must realise that any new retreat on their part is unacceptable, that they must not retreat any further.

Andropov: Jaruzelski has been getting everything off his chest and Kania, lately, has been hitting the bottle. It is all very sad ... The situation in Poland is influencing the western regions of our country. In Belorussia, in particular, where many villages can pick up Polish radio and TV. It should also be added that in some other regions, such as Georgia, there have been spontaneous demonstrations, groups of loudmouths have assembled in the street, as recently in Tbilisi [capital of Georgia], and shouted anti-Soviet slogans. Here as well, domestically, we shall have to take severe measures.

Boukovsky [7], pp. 442–4.

(b) By the end of 1981, Moscow had changed its mind. It was up to the Poles to decide for themselves what to do. Under no circumstances would Moscow intervene militarily in Poland. At a meeting on 10 December 1981, the Politburo was unclear what Jaruzelski had in mind, only three days before he proclaimed martial law in Poland.

Andropov: Our position, formulated at the previous meeting of the Politburo and expressed many times by L. I. Brezhnev, is absolutely correct and we may not deviate from it. In other words, we have adopted the position of international aid, we are disturbed by the situation which has arisen in Poland, but, as regards operation X [military measures], this is absolutely and completely the responsibility of our Polish comrades, whatever they decide will be fine. We shall not insist on anything and not dissuade them from doing anything ...
If comrade Kulikov [Warsaw Pact commander, a Russian] has actually spoken of the sending of troops, I think that he has acted incorrectly. We cannot take any risks. We are not inclined to send troops to Poland. This is a correct attitude, and we need to hold to it. I do not know what will happen in Poland, but even if it falls to a Solidarity coup, that would be something. Otherwise the capitalist countries would hurl themselves at the Soviet Union, and they have already reached all types of agreements to impose all kinds of economic and political sanctions on our country. This would be very painful for us. We have to look after our own country and strengthen the Soviet Union ... As regards the lines of communications between the Soviet Union and east Germany across Polish territory, of course, we must do something to protect them.

Boukovsky [7], p. 454.

(c)
Jaruzelski kept on requesting all kinds of aid and there were those in the Politburo who thought he was playing a tactical game. If he failed to get aid, he could blame the Russians for the shortages in Poland. However, some meat was being sent. Baibakov, chair of Gosplan, reports, on 10 December 1981, about the fate of the Polish meat. Poland was expensive.

One estimate put the cost to Russia, in 1981 alone, at US$2.9 billion. This extract reveals that the Poles no longer feared the Russians. They enjoyed baiting the Russian bear. This is a prelude to the collapse of the Soviet empire in eastern Europe at the end of the 1980s.

As you know, according to the instructions of the Politburo and the request of our Polish comrades, we had to deliver 30,000 tonnes of meat to them. 16,000 tonnes of this has already crossed the frontier. It should be pointed out that ... the meat has been delivered in dirty wagons, wagons which had previously carried ore, and had not been cleaned, and that it looked rather pathetic. Sabotage occurred during the unloading of this meat at Polish stations. The Poles expressed themselves in the most inappropriate manner about the Soviet Union and its inhabitants, they refused to unload the wagons, etc. It would be impossible to count the number of insults which showered down on us.

Boukovsky [7], pp. 459–60.

DOCUMENT 11   A TOP ADVISER'S WITHERING CRITICISM
OF SOVIET FOREIGN POLICY

(a) Vyacheslav Dashichev, the leading German specialist in the Academy of Sciences, provided situation papers on various aspects of Soviet foreign policy. On 22 April 1982 his institute submitted the following document by him, 'An Analysis of the Present State of East–West Relations', to the Party Central Committee. As he later wrote, the 'dangerous and irresponsible' policies undertaken by the Brezhnev leadership 'shocked' him. Brezhnev, as far as is known, did not react to this report.

The intervention of our troops in Afghanistan, without any doubt, overstepped the permissible limits of the east–west confrontation in the Third World. The advantages of such a move are nothing compared to the disadvantages:

- The Soviet Union created a dangerous, third front – after that in [eastern] Europe against [western] Europe and in east Asia against China – on its southern flank under very unfavourable geographical and socio-political conditions. Here we shall have to contend with the combined resources of the USA, NATO and China as well and the Islamic countries and the Afghan feudal-clerical insurgent army, which has imposed great pressure on the Afghan people. We face, for the first time since the Second World War, the possibility of a local military conflict, in which we, in contrast to the Korean, Vietnamese and other wars, will have to fight with our own troops. As a result, the threat of a military escalation increases.

- The number of anti-Soviet states has significantly increased and consolidated.
- The influence of the USSR on the non-aligned movement, especially the Islamic world, has sharply fallen.
- Détente has been blocked and the prerequisites for arms control are no longer present.
- The economic and technological pressure on the Soviet Union has risen sharply.
- Western and Chinese propaganda have been presented with great opportunities to step up the campaign to undermine the standing of the Soviet Union in the west, the Third World and socialist states.
- The events in Afghanistan, coupled with those in Cambodia, have nullified the possible normalisation of Sino-Soviet relations.
- These events could act as a catalyst to overcome the crisis in relations between Iran and the USA and for their reconciliation.
- Mistrust of Soviet policy has increased and Yugoslavia, China and Romania have become more distant. For the first time, the Hungarian and Polish mass media have been less than supportive of Soviet policy in Afghanistan. This is manifested by the mood of the public and the fear of the leaderships of these countries that they could become involved in the world-wide policies of the Soviet Union. Our partners, due to the limitations of their resources, are not equipped for such a struggle.
- The western powers are increasingly adopting differing policies. They have adopted a new tactic, that of interfering actively in Soviet relations with socialist countries and of concentrating on conflicts and their different interests.
- The Soviet Union faces a new economic burden. The escalation of the conflict between the Soviet Union and the west, and China in the Third World, brought into question, at the end of the 1970s, the most important achievements of détente. The continued expansion of our military-political offensive in the Third World will be countered by the west by moving more and more towards a 'cold' or 'semi-cold' war and increasing pressure on the Soviet Union in the political, economic, military-strategic and propaganda-psychological spheres. A gradual return to détente could be achieved by abandoning our military commitments in the Third World, but only if the crisis does not spread to other regions, in particular, eastern Europe.

Dashichev [36], pp. 219–21.

(b) Dashichev knew Andropov quite well and their children were friends. He felt, for the first time, that he could speak his mind about the follies of Soviet foreign policy and submitted the following situation report to the new General Secretary on 10 January 1983. It is a devastating indictment of Soviet policy and warns of the risks of nuclear war. Some of the concepts were later adopted by Gorbachev.

If a great power sets out to expand rapidly its influence and its sphere of hegemonic power, what would be the consequences for the world community? Weak countries would be forced to submit to the dominance of the great power. It would thereby become stronger and would oblige larger and larger states to accept its rule until the whole world had become one super state or be ruled by this super state. But this has yet to occur. The reason for this is that in the world community there is the law of the 'automatic repercussions [or reactions]', which acts to contain the expansion of the great power and opposes the extension of its dominance. This occurs when its power oversteps certain limits and begins to threaten the interests of other states, especially those of the great powers.

The result of the 'automatic repercussions' promotes the formation of a 'counter-coalition' of powerful states to oppose the potential or actual strongest state. The level of the 'repercussions' is the result of its appropriateness or its over-reaction, i.e. the growth of an expansionist great power at a particular time will either be blocked, or through the setting up of a stronger coalition, will be decisively weakened. The latter results in practice from a growth in power, the consequence of new states joining the 'counter-coalition' and mobilising their whole material, spiritual and human resources ...

Events have underlined the invalidity of the assertion that countries which have embarked on the road of socialist development would recognise the leading role of the Soviet Union. Also that relations between the Soviet Union and other socialist states could be based, on the international level, on the intra-party principle of democratic centralism. It transpired that the hegemonic role [of the Soviet Union] – irrespective of whatever slogan was chosen – provoked a reaction from the capitalist but also – in no less extent – from socialist countries. In the immediate post war years it was difficult to conceive of some socialist states opposing the Soviet Union. These turned out to be Yugoslavia, China, Albania, and to a certain extent, North Korea and Romania. It was even more unlikely that socialist China would cooperate with the 'counter-coalition' ...

Détente presented the Soviet Union with rare opportunities:

- To demonstrate its determination to reduce the conflict with the west to the barest minimum so as to prevent the strengthening of the 'counter-coalition'.

- To direct all its energy and resources to the development of the socio-economic potential of the country, to switch the economy to intensive development, which would reduce the level of the 'automatic repercussions' and weaken the 'counter-coalition'.

- To build up the hinterland and strengthen the whole system of relations and cooperation within Comecon and the Warsaw Pact, based on a socialist partnership.

- To seek new ways and forms of support for national liberation movements which would not undermine détente.

Unfortunately these chances were missed and the Soviet Union was subjected to an unprecedented attack by the imperialists. This policy turn will cost [the USSR], in the five years 1981–6, (only to be compared with the military budget of the USA), US$1.5 trillion, if not more. This has resulted in a dangerous growth of military tension …

From the western point of view, the expansion of the Soviet zone of influence in the post-war period reached a critical point with the invasion of Afghanistan by Soviet troops. Previously that could have led to the 'counter-coalition' beginning a war. However the danger of mutual annihilation prevented the west from launching a full frontal attack on the Soviet Union. Since nuclear war was not a rational means of attaining political goals, the 'counter-coalition' adopted other means of pressure. The massive expansion in defence spending, the maximum damage to the Soviet economy, the goal of military-strategic superiority and the concentration of the spiritual and material resources of the capitalist world, are among the most important.

The contemporary policy of the USA and its allies can be labelled 'excessive repercussions [or overreactions]'. This means that the world is now in an extremely dangerous, critical period which can lead to a new world war. The hopes of nuclear deterrence and certain nuclear annihilation serving as factors to prevent war may prove to be fatal illusions …

The Soviet Union is now in an extremely difficult position. Almost all the great powers of the world, except India, have lined up against it. Resisting their vastly greater potential is dangerously way beyond the potential of the Soviet Union.

Ways of reducing the 'excessive' pressure of the 'counter-coalition' on the Soviet Union is the main concern at present of Soviet foreign policy. It is perfectly clear that this task can only be achieved by gradual self-limitation and careful behaviour on the world stage by the Soviet Union.

Under present circumstances, the Soviet Union can no longer act as the guarantor and protector of the revolutionary and national liberation movements. This mission is beyond the Soviet Union. A fundamental reorientation of our behaviour on the international stage is now necessary … this is the only possibility to arrest and neutralise the processes which, if they get out of control, will inevitably result in a nuclear war …

It is also clear that it is impossible to *solve the problem of restraining the arms race and reducing the risk of war by merely engaging in military negotiations without fundamentally changing political relations between the USSR and the west.* The key question is not, at the end of the day, about the quantity and quality of the weapons one side has but to what extent a political modus vivendi is possible between the Soviet Union and the western powers. Precisely here, in the political sphere, is to be found the key to solving the problem of disarmament and the reduction of the risk of war.

Dashichev [36], pp. 224–32.

DOCUMENT 12   GORBACHEV'S NEW THINKING

Gorbachev's astonishing innovations in foreign policy transformed the world. Here he admits that the Soviet Union had been going up a blind ally for decades. The time was ripe for Moscow to emerge from its self-imposed isolation and join the rest of the world. This momentous decision meant the end of a class-based foreign policy. Henceforth, the common interests of mankind would take preference over the interests of the working class. This was very controversial and Ligachev, for one, strongly opposed this policy change.

In late May 1986, we discussed the new role of Soviet diplomacy at a conference held at the Ministry of Foreign Affairs ... The Minister of Foreign Affairs [Shevardnadze] made a speech which was then discussed by the participants, and I later addressed the conference. The gist of my speech was the lagging behind of our international agencies, which did not keep up with the policies and practical steps undertaken by the country's political leadership. Today I consider this meeting the starting point for the full scale implementation of our 'new thinking'.

We realised it was vitally necessary to correct the distorted ideas we had about other nations. These misconceptions had made us oppose the rest of the world for many decades, which had negative effects on our economy as well as on the public consciousness, science, culture and the intellectual potential of our country.

We understand that in today's world of mutual interdependence, progress is unthinkable for any society which is fenced off from the world by impenetrable state frontiers and ideological barriers. A country can develop its full potential by interacting with other societies, yet without giving up its own identity.

We realised that we could not ensure our country's security without reckoning with the interests of other countries, and that, in our nuclear age, you could not build a safe security system based solely on military means. This prompted us to propose an entirely new concept of global security, which included all aspects of international relations, including the human dimension.

Gorbachev [25], pp. 402–3.

DOCUMENT 13   THE REYKJAVIK SUMMIT

Gorbachev and Reagan almost achieved a sensational breakthrough in arms control at the summit. It foundered on SDI, on which Reagan would not budge. At a Politburo meeting on 22 October 1986 Gorbachev gives vent to his frustrations.

Gorbachev: We have to alter our views on the measures connected to the latest hostile behaviour by the American administration. The turn of events since Reykjavik reveals that our 'friends' in the United States lack any positive programme and are doing everything to increase pressure on us. And into the bargain, with extreme brutality, and are conducting themselves like true bandits.

Solomentsev: Yes, they are behaving like really big bandits.

Gorbachev: It is quite impossible to expect the American administration to do anything or come up with anything constructive. At present, we have to score propaganda points, continue our media offensive directed at American and international public opinion. The leaders in Washington are afraid of that. Customs have blocked for three days my statements for Reykjavik and Soviet TV.

Yakovlev: Comrade Bugaev telephoned me to say that these texts are still being held up by the American customs.

Gorbachev: We have to keep on applying pressure on the American administration by explaining our positions to the public and demonstrate that the responsibility for the failure to agree on the limitation and liquidation of nuclear armaments rests fairly and squarely with the Americans.

Boukovsky [7], pp. 482–3.

DOCUMENT 14   GORBACHEV, REAGAN AND SDI

President Reagan was a strong believer in SDI, and Gorbachev did his best, at Geneva, to wean him away from it.

Ronald Reagan's advocacy of the Strategic Defence Initiative struck me as bizarre. Was it science fiction, a trick to make the Soviet Union more forthcoming, or merely a crude attempt to lull us in order to carry out the mad enterprise – the creation of a shield which would allow a first strike without fear of retaliation? Yet I had consulted scientists on the issue beforehand, and the volley of arguments which President Reagan launched at me did not catch me unprepared. My answer was sharp and strong. I said that Mr. Reagan's words simply proved that the Americans mistrusted us. Why should we trust them any more than they trusted us?

'SDI is the continuation of the arms race into a different, more dangerous sphere', I continued. 'It will only foment mistrust and suspicion, with each side fearing the other is overtaking it. The Soviet Union strongly opposes an arms race in space ... I think you should know that we have already developed a response. It will be effective and far less expensive than your project, and be ready for use in less time.' ... I can assure you that we were not bluffing. Our studies had proved that the potential answer to SDI could meet the requirements I had mentioned.

Gorbachev [25], p. 407.

DOCUMENT 15   **GORBACHEV AND MRS THATCHER**

Gorbachev's first meeting with Mrs Thatcher, the British Prime Minister, in December 1984, had been a success. The two were to develop a special relationship during the perestroika years.

Mrs. Thatcher came to Moscow in late March 1987 ... Stressing the significance of her visit, I remarked that the last high level visit to the Soviet Union by a British Prime Minister had taken place more than twelve years earlier. She corrected me immediately, saying that the last time a British *Conservative* Prime Minister had visited the Soviet Union had been more than twenty years before ...

Mrs. Thatcher had maintained that the Soviet Union aspired to 'establish communism and domination worldwide' and that 'Moscow's hand' could be seen in virtually every conflict in the world. Obviously I could not leave it at that and replied that much of her speech in Torquay [a week before] as well as most of the accusations she had made were conservative stereotypes going back to the 1940s and 1950s. But Mrs. Thatcher stood her ground. 'You are supplying weapons to the Third World countries', she rejoined, 'while the West supplies them with food and aid in addition to helping establish democratic institutions.' The discussion became very heated.

Our discussion had reached a point where I considered it necessary to say: 'We have frankly expressed our respective views on the world in which we live. But we have not succeeded in bringing the standpoints any closer. It seems to me that our disagreements have not become less after this conversation.'

My partner struck a more conciliatory note. Suddenly changing the course of our conversation, she said: 'We follow your activity with great interest and we fully appreciate your attempts to improve the life of your people. I acknowledge your right to have your own system and security, just as we have the right to ours, and we suggest taking this as a basis for our debate.

'In spite of all the differences between our systems', she added, 'we can exchange some useful experiences. We are deeply impressed by the vigorous policy of reform you are trying to implement. We have a common problem here – how to manage change.'

Mrs. Thatcher advanced the familiar argument that nuclear weapons represented the best guarantee for peace and that there could be no other guarantee in present conditions. 'We believe in nuclear deterrence', she continued, 'and we do not consider the elimination of nuclear weapons practicable.'

In reply I delivered quite a long harangue ... 'Today, we are closer than ever before to making a first step towards genuine disarmament. But the moment we were given this opportunity, you hit the panic button ...'

Mrs. Thatcher seemed somewhat taken aback by my tirade. 'That's what I call a speech!', she exclaimed, 'I don't even know where to start.'

Gorbachev [25], pp. 434–5.

DOCUMENT 16   MOSCOW AND FRATERNAL PARTIES

(a) The CC Secretariat, on 18 January 1989, discussed a request from Colonel Quadaffi, the Libyan leader. It resolved that the Ministry of Defence was to receive, in 1990, 20 Libyan terrorists for 'special military training'. In April 1989 a CC document revealed the extent of the training of comrades from non-socialist countries.

Secret Confidential
Special Dossier

No. St–99/248 gs
10 April 1989

Resolution of the CC Secretariat, CPSU

The leadership of several fraternal parties in non-socialist countries every year request the CC to accept their activists for special training. During the last ten years, over 500 full time Party officials from 40 communist and workers' parties (including members of their Politburos and CC) have received instruction. According to the decision of the CC, the international department has been responsible for welcoming and looking after them, and the KGB for providing their training.

[Signed: [Aleksandr] Yakovlev]

Boukovsky [7], p. 495.

(b) Despite the espousal of universal human values, Gorbachev's Soviet Union continued to fund communist parties around the globe until 1990. A hilarious episode, at least to the outsider, was the case of Luis Corvalán, the former leader of the Communist Party of Chile, who had been living illegally in Chile since 1983, 'with a different face', while conducting the communist struggle against General Pinochet. Corvalán requested the CC to help him to become legal again. There was no need to stay in hiding since Pinochet had called elections and lost them. However, there was a problem. Corvalán had undergone plastic surgery so as to go unrecognised in Chile. He needed to return clandestinely to the Soviet Union, have plastic surgery to restore his original face, and obtain a legal passport. The Communist Party of Chile requested the CC to arrange for comrade Corvalán to be eased into a western country where he could go to the Chilean embassy to obtain a valid passport. While waiting, he had to leave Chile unrecognised, so he needed another new face to leave!

Secret Confidential
Special Dossier

No. St–112/27 gs
14 February 1990

Resolution of the CC Secretariat, CPSU

1) Partially fulfil the request of the leaderships of the Communist Parties of Argentina and Chile and welcome to the Soviet Union, in 1990, for a period of up to three months, five members of the Communist Party of Argentina and four members of the Communist Party of Chile, seeking instruction in the security of the Party and its leaders, based particularly on technical means.

2) Reception and maintenance of these comrades will be the responsibility of the international department of the CC, CPSU. Their training, provision of documents and special equipment will be the duty of the KGB.

Boukovsky [7], p. 494.

CHRONOLOGY

1949   4 April: NATO is set up in Washington.
        4 May: Four-power agreement in New York on the
                           ending of the Berlin blockade to be effective
                           on 12 May.
        25 September: Tass reports on the explosion of the first So-
                           viet atomic bomb.

1950   31 January: President Truman announces that the US is
                           to build a hydrogen bomb.
        25 June: The Korean War begins.
        27 June: UN, with the USSR absent, approves the
                           uniting for peace resolution to send troops
                           to Korea.

1951   10 March: The Soviet Union, in notes to the western
                           powers, proposes a peace treaty with Ger-
                           many.

1952   3 October: Britain explodes its first atomic bomb suc-
                           cessfully in the Montebello Islands.
        1 November: The US explodes its first hydrogen bomb
                           successfully in the Marshall Islands.

1953   5 March: Stalin dies from a heart attack suffered on 1
                           March.
        20 August: The Soviet Union announces the explosion
                           of a hydrogen bomb (explosion was on 8
                           August).
        13 September: Nikita Khrushchev is elected First Secretary
                           of the Communist Party.

1954	1 March:	The US tests the first deliverable hydrogen bomb in the Marshall Islands.
	26 April– 21 July:	The Indo-China conference in Geneva of the foreign ministers of the Soviet Union, France, Great Britain and the US agree on the division of Vietnam along the 17th parallel.
	7 May:	Dien Bien Phu falls to the Viet-Minh, the day before the Geneva talks were to discuss Indo-China. This defeat heralds the end of French influence in Indo-China.
1955	18–24 April:	Bandung conference in Indonesia of Afro-Asian states; condemns racism and colonialism.
	14 May:	In Warsaw, the Soviet Union and Albania, Bulgaria, Hungary, the GDR, Poland, Romania and Czechoslovakia sign a treaty for the defence of peace and security in Europe for 20 years (known as the Warsaw Pact). After ratification it becomes operative on 5 June 1955.
	15 May:	The four powers and Austria sign in Vienna the Austrian state treaty which confirms the state frontiers of 1 January 1938 and Austria agrees not to conclude a political or economic union with Germany. Austria is to be a neutral country.
1956	17 April:	The Cominform is dissolved and to be replaced by bilateral agreements between the Soviet Union and the individual states.
	23 October– 11 November:	The Hungarian Revolution; after the attack by Israel against the Suez Canal (29 October) the Soviet Union issues a sharp warning to Israel, France and Great Britain.
	5 November:	The Soviet Union severs diplomatic relations with Israel and threatens France and Great Britain because of their troop landings in Suez (5 November), not excluding a rocket attack against London and Paris.

1957	5 January:	President Eisenhower, in an address to Congress, commits the US to oppose communism in the Middle East, called the Eisenhower doctrine. Adopted on 9 March.
	19 September:	The US explodes its first nuclear device underground in Nevada.
	4 October:	The launch of Sputnik by the Soviet Union begins the era of space travel.
	15 October:	Secret agreement between the Soviet Union and China which provides Soviet help for the development of Chinese nuclear weapons. The agreement is cancelled by Moscow on 20 June 1959.
	3 November:	Launch of Sputnik 2 with the dog Laika on board. It is the first time a living creature has been sent into space.
1958	27 November:	First Soviet ultimatum on Berlin. The Soviet Union withdraws from the agreement on the administration of Greater Berlin (12 September 1944), on the Control Council (1 May 1945) and its responsibilities under the 20 September 1955 treaty with the GDR. All the rights and duties in these agreements are transferred to the GDR government. West Berlin should become a demilitarised Free City. Khrushchev demands that Berlin problem be resolved within six months.
1959	2 January:	Launch of Lunik, the first Soviet two-stage rocket which passes the moon on 4 January at a distance of 7,500km and becomes the first satellite of the sun.
	14 September:	The Luna 2 space station lands on the moon (launched on 12 September).
	15–27 September:	Khrushchev's first visit to the US. He meets President Eisenhower at Camp David (26–27 September) and withdraws his Berlin ultimatum and this leads to the Camp David spirit emerging.

1960	5 May:	Moscow announces the shooting down of the US U2 spy plane, piloted by Gary Powers.
	16–17 May:	The U2 incident results in the Paris summit failing when Khrushchev demands that President Eisenhower apologise for the incident.
	19 September–30 October:	Khrushchev attends the UN, addresses the General Assembly several times, and thumps his desk during a speech by Macmillan (29 September) and bangs on his desk with a shoe during a speech by the Philippine delegate (12 October).
1961	20 January:	During his inauguration, President Kennedy states that the US will 'pay any price, bear any burden, meet any hardship, support any friend, oppose any foe, to ensure the survival and the success of liberty'.
	12 April:	Yury Gagarin, in Vostok 1, becomes the first person to circle the earth.
	17–20 April:	The Bay of Pigs invasion by Cuban exiles, backed by the CIA, is a disastrous failure.
	3–4 June:	Khrushchev and President John F. Kennedy meet in Vienna. Khrushchev demands the demilitarisation of Berlin.
	13 August:	The building of the Berlin Wall begins.
1962	25 September–7 January 1963:	The Cuban missile crisis.
1963	14 June–14 July:	The Communist Party of China forwards an open letter to Moscow accusing the Russians of 'restoring capitalism' and betraying Marxism. The treaty on nuclear weapons of 15 October 1957 is annulled by the Russians.
1964	14 October:	Nikita Khrushchev is removed as First Secretary of the Communist Party. Leonid Brezhnev is elected Party leader and Aleksei Kosygin Prime Minister.

1966	10 January:	Kosygin helps to bring the Indian-Pakistani conflict to an end and both sides sign an agreement in Tashkent. This is a coup for Soviet influence in Asia and helps to stem the increase in Chinese influence.
1968	21 August:	Invasion of Czechoslovakia by Warsaw Pact forces, headed by the Soviet Union, with smaller contingents from the GDR, Poland, Hungary and Bulgaria. Romania, Yugoslavia, China and Albania protest against the invasion.
	12 November:	Leonid Brezhnev, in Warsaw, introduces the Brezhnev doctrine of limited sovereignty of communist pro-Moscow states.
1969	2 March:	Armed conflict between Chinese and Soviet forces on the islands in the Ussuri river. There is further fighting on 14–15 March.
	17 April:	More Soviet-Chinese fighting along the Xinjiang border with Central Asia.
1970	12 August:	Aleksei Kosygin and Andrei Gromyko, Soviet Foreign Minister, and Chancellor Willy Brandt and Walter Scheel, West German Foreign Minister, sign the Soviet-West German Moscow treaty which begins Bonn's Ostpolitik. This states that European frontiers can only be changed by negotiation. The treaty is followed by the Warsaw treaty of 7 December 1970.
1971	3 September:	Four power Berlin treaty regulates the status of west Berlin (transit of civil goods and persons, expansion of links with West Germany, representation of west Berlin abroad). After GDR–West German agreements, a final protocol is added on 3 June 1972.

1972   22–30 May: Official state visit by President Richard Nixon to the Soviet Union, during which the SALT treaty is signed (26 May).

3 October: President Nixon and Andrei Gromyko sign the Anti-Ballistic Missile (ABM) treaty.

1973   18–25 June: During the visit of Leonid Brezhnev to the United States agreement is reached on the basic principles of talks cutting back further on strategic offensive weapons (21 June) and avoiding military confrontation and a missile war (22 June).

1974   27 June–3 July: During the visit of President Nixon to the Soviet Union several agreements on limiting strategic arms and co-operation between the two countries are signed.

24 November: During a meeting between Leonid Brezhnev and President Gerald Ford in Vladivostok, it is agreed to conclude a treaty on limiting strategic arms over the period October 1977 to December 1985.

1975   1 August: The Helsinki Final Act is signed by heads of states and governments.

1–5 December: President Ford visits China and meets Mao Zedong, who criticises US-Soviet détente.

1976   6–26 September: Arthur Schlesinger, a former US secretary of state, visits China and offers Beijing an alliance against the Soviet Union and analyses the weaknesses of the Chinese air defence system.

1979   15–18 June: SALT II is signed at a Soviet-US summit in Vienna between President Carter and Leonid Brezhnev.

12 December: In response to the stationing of SS 20 medium-range missiles in the western regions of the Soviet Union, the NATO states agree, in Brussels, to station American Cruise and Pershing 2 missiles in western Europe from 1984.

1979	26–27 December:	Soviet troops intervene in Afghanistan.
1980	4 January:	In response to the Soviet invasion of Afghanistan, President Jimmy Carter imposes a trade embargo for grain and advanced technology; he also suspends the ratification of the SALT II treaty and promises greater aid to Pakistan.
1981	6 August:	President Reagan announces the stockpiling of neutron bombs by the US.
1982	30 May:	President Reagan promises that the US will adhere to SALT II as long as the Soviet Union does.
	10 November:	Leonid Brezhnev dies.
	12 November:	Yury Andropov is elected General Secretary of the Communist Party.
1983	9 March:	President Reagan describes the Soviet Union as the 'evil empire'.
	23 March:	President Reagan announces the Strategic Defence Initiative (SDI), also called the Star Wars programme.
1984	9 February:	Yury Andropov dies.
	13 February:	Konstantin Chernenko is elected General Secretary of the Communist Party.
	15–21 December:	Mikhail Gorbachev visits Great Britain and Mrs Margaret Thatcher, Prime Minister, regards him as a man with whom one can do business.
1985	10 March:	Konstantin Chernenko dies.
	11 March:	Mikhail Gorbachev is elected General Secretary of the Communist Party.
	2 July:	Eduard Shevardnadze succeeds Andrei Gromyko as Foreign Minister.
	19–21 November:	Summit meeting in Geneva between Mikhail Gorbachev and President Ronald Reagan and they agree to meet in the future.

1986	25 February– 6 March:	The 27th Party Congress opens with a long keynote speech by Gorbachev. He refers to the war in Afghanistan as a 'bleeding wound' and the Brezhnev era as 'years of stagnation'.
	10 October:	Gorbachev arrives in Reykjavik for a two-day summit with President Reagan. They agree on most arms reduction issues. They almost agree on substantial cuts in offensive arms and even the elimination of nuclear weapons.
	28 November:	The US deploys the new B52 bomber which violates the START II treaty.
1987	28 March– 1 April:	British Prime Minister, Margaret Thatcher, visits the Soviet Union and stresses human rights and calls for the withdrawal of Soviet troops from Afghanistan.
	5 December:	Gorbachev travels to London and meets Margaret Thatcher.
	7–10 December:	Gorbachev visits Washington for meetings with President Ronald Reagan and they sign the treaty banning intermediate-range nuclear missiles (INF) (8 December). It is his first visit to the United States and becomes a huge personal triumph; Gorbymania has appeared.
1988	14 April:	Agreements on the ending of the Afghan war are signed in Geneva.
	29 May– 2 June:	President Reagan visits Moscow to meet Gorbachev for their fourth summit.
	7 December:	Gorbachev, at the UN, announces that the Soviet Union will reduce its armed forces by 500,000 within two years without requiring reciprocal moves by the US or its allies. Later he meets Reagan and President-elect Bush on Governors Island.
1989	15 February:	The last Soviet troops leave Afghanistan.
	15–19 May:	Gorbachev visits China and announces the normalisation of relations between the two states.

1989	6 July:	Gorbachev addresses the Council of Europe in Strasbourg and states that the Soviet Union will not stand in the way of reform in eastern Europe.
	7 October:	Gorbachev, in east Berlin, tells the crowds that 'life punishes those who fall behind' and this further undermines the authority of Erich Honecker, the GDR leader. He is replaced by Egon Krenz on 18 October.
	9 November:	The Berlin Wall comes down.
	2–3 December:	Gorbachev and Bush meet in Malta and Gorbachev states that force will not be used to ensure that east European communist regimes remain in power. Bush agrees to remove most controls on US-Soviet trade.
1990	8 February:	James Baker visits Moscow and proposes 2 (East and West Germany) + 4 (the US, USSR, Britain and France) negotiations to discuss German unification.
	30 May–4 June:	Gorbachev travels to Washington for his second summit with Bush, then visits Minneapolis-St Paul and San Francisco.
	August 2:	Iraq invades Kuwait.
	9 September:	Gorbachev and Bush meet for a one-day summit in Helsinki and agree to co-operate to end Iraqi aggression in Kuwait.
	12 September:	The 2 + 4 treaty is signed in Moscow ending four-power control over Germany.
	3 October:	Germany is reunited.
	19 November:	The treaty on Conventional Forces in Europe (CFE) is signed in Paris.
	20 December:	Eduard Shevardnadze, Minister of Foreign Affairs, resigns and warns of the threat of dictatorship.
1991	15 January:	Operation Desert Storm, to remove Iraq from Kuwait, begins in the Persian Gulf.
	31 March:	The Warsaw Pact is formally dissolved.
	20 June:	The US ambassador warns Gorbachev of a conspiracy to remove him.

1991	30 June:	The last Soviet soldier leaves Czechoslovakia (they had invaded on 21 August 1968).
	30–31 July:	President Bush visits Moscow, meets Gorbachev and Nazarbaev, and pays a separate visit to Yeltsin.
	1 August:	President Bush visits Kiev and meets Leonid Kravchuk.
	19 August:	The Emergency Committee announces that it has assumed power and demands that all institutions obey its orders.
	21 August:	The attempted coup fails; Gorbachev returns to Moscow.
	8 December:	In Belovezh forest, near Minsk, the Presidents and Prime Ministers of Russia, Ukraine and Belarus declare the USSR dissolved and found a Commonwealth of Independent States (CIS). Gorbachev describes the move 'dangerous and illegal'.
	21–22 December:	Eleven former Soviet republics meet in Almaty and the CIS is extended (Estonia, Latvia, Lithuania and Georgia did not attend).
	25 December:	USSR President Gorbachev resigns and the Russian flag replaces the Soviet flag over the Kremlin.
	27 December:	President Yeltsin takes over President Gorbachev's office in the Kremlin.
	31 December:	The Soviet Union ceases to exist in international law.

BIBLIOGRAPHY

1 Ashton, S. R., *The Politics of East–West Relations Since 1945*, Macmillan, London, 1989.
2 Baker, James A. III, *The Politics of Diplomacy: Revolution, War and Peace*, G. P. Putnam's, New York, 1995.
3 Beschloss, Michael R., *Kennedy v. Khrushchev, The Crisis Years 1960–63*, Faber and Faber, London, 1991.
4 Beschloss, Michael, and Strobe Talbott, *The Inside Story of the End of the Cold War*, Little, Brown, London, 1993.
5 Bialer, Seweryn, *Politics, Society, and Nationality Inside Gorbachev's Russia*, Westview, Boulder, CO, 1989.
6 Borg, Dorothy, and Waldo Heinrichs, *Uncertain Years: Chinese-American Relations, 1947–1950*, Columbia University Press, New York, 1980.
7 Boukovsky, Vladimir, *Jugement à Moscou. Un Dissident dans les Archives du Kremlin*, Robert Laffont, Paris, 1995.
8 Brzezinski, Zbigniew, *Power and Principle*, Weidenfeld and Nicolson, London, 1983.
9 Cohen, Warren I., *America in the Age of Soviet Power, 1945–1991*, Cambridge University Press, Cambridge, 1993.
10 Cohen Warren, *Dean Rusk*, Cooper Square Publishers, Totowa, NJ, 1980.
11 Cohen, Warren I., and Akira Iriye, eds, *The Great Powers in East Asia, 1953–1960*, New York, 1990.
12 Cumings, Bruce, *The Origins of the Korean War*, 2 vols, Princeton University Press, Princeton, NJ, 1981, 1990.
13 Dobrynin, Anatoly, *In Confidence: Moscow's Ambassador to America's Six Cold War Presidents*, Random House, New York, 1995.
14 Duggan, Christopher, and Christopher Wagstaff, eds, *Italy in the Cold War: Politics, Culture and Society 1948–58*, Berg, Oxford, 1995.
15 Ekedahl, Caroline McGiffert, and Melvin A. Goodman, *The Wars of Eduard Shevardnadze*, Hurst, London, 1997.
16 Gaddis, John Lewis, *Russia, the Soviet Union and the United States*, 2nd edn, McGraw-Hill, New York, 1990.
17 Gaddis, John Lewis, *The Long Peace: Inquiries into the History of the Cold War*, Oxford University Press, Oxford, 1987.

18   Garthoff, Raymond L., *Détente and Confrontation, American-Soviet Relations from Nixon to Reagan,* rev. edn, The Brookings Institution, Washington, DC, 1994.
19   Garthoff, Raymond, *Reflections on the Cuban Missile Crisis,* rev. edn, The Brookings Institution, Washington, DC, 1989.
20   Garver, John W., *China's Decision for Rapprochement with the United States, 1968–1971,* Westview, Boulder, CO, 1982.
21   Gelman, Harry, *The Brezhnev Politburo and the Decline of Détente,* Cornell University Press, Ithaca, 1984.
22   Gilpin, Robert, *The Political Economy of International Relations,* Princeton University Press, Princeton, NJ, 1987.
23   Goldman, Eric, *The Crucial Decade – and After,1945–1960,* Alfred A. Knopf, New York, 1971.
24   Gorbachev, Mikhail, *Perestroika: New Thinking for Our Country and the World,* Collins, London, 1987.
25   Gorbachev, Mikhail, *Memoirs,* Doubleday, London, 1996.
26   Graham, Billy, *Just as I Am,* Harper, San Francisco, 1997.
27   Halliday, Fred, *The Making of the Second Cold War,* Verso, London, 1983.
28   Hamilton, Nora et al., *Crisis in Central America,* Westview, Boulder, CO, 1988.
29   Harding, Harry, *A Fragile Relationship: The United States and China Since 1972,* The Brookings Institution, Washington, DC, 1992.
30   Harrison, Hope M., 'New Evidence on Khrushchev's 1958 Berlin Ultimatum', *Cold War International History Project Bulletin,* Woodrow Wilson Center, Washington, DC, no. 4, Autumn, 1994.
31   Harrison, Hope M., 'Ulbricht and the Concrete "Rose". New Archival Evidence on the Dynamics of Soviet-East German Relations and the Berlin Crisis, 1958–1961', Working Paper no. 5, Cold War International History Project, Woodrow Wilson Center, Washington, DC, May 1993.
32   Herring, George, *America's Longest War,* 2nd edn, McGraw-Hill, New York, 1986 [on Vietnam].
33   Hogan, Michael J., *The Marshall Plan,* Cambridge University Press, Cambridge, 1990.
34   Holloway, David, *The Soviet Union and the Arms Race,* 2nd edn, Yale University Press, New Haven, 1984.
35   Hough, Jerry, *The Struggle for the Third World,* The Brookings Institution, Washington, DC, 1986.
36   *Jahrbuch für Historische Kommunismusforschung,* Akademie Verlag, Berlin, 1997.
37   Jervis, Robert, *The Meaning of the Nuclear Revolution,* Cornell University Press, Ithaca, 1989.
38   Kahin, A. *Intervention,* New York, 1986 [on Indo-China].
39   Kaplan, Lawrence, *NATO and the United States,* updated edn, Twayne Publishers, Boston, 1994.

40   Kelleher, Catherine, *Germany and the Politics of Nuclear Weapons*, New York, 1975.
41   Kennedy, Paul, *The Rise and Fall of the Great Powers*, Fontana, London, 1989.
42   Khrushchev, Nikita, *Khrushchev Remembers*, with an introduction, commentary and notes by Edward Chankshaw, trans. by Strobe Talbott, Sphere Books, London, 1971.
43   Khrushchev, Nikita, *Khrushchev Remembers*, vol. 1, trans. and ed. by Strobe Talbott, Little Brown, Boston, 1970.
44   Khrushchev, Nikita, *Khrushchev Remembers: The Last Testament*, vol. 2, trans. and ed. by Strobe Talbott, Little Brown, Boston, 1974.
45   Khrushchev, Nikita, *Khrushchev Remembers: The Glasnost Tapes*, with a foreword by Strobe Talbott, trans. and ed. by Jerrold L. Schecter and Vyacheslav V. Luchkov, Little Brown, Boston, 1974.
46   Kissinger, Henry, *The White House Years*, Weidenfeld and Nicolson, London, 1979.
47   Kissinger, Henry, *Years of Upheaval*, Weidenfeld and Nicolson, London, 1982.
48   LaFeber, Walter, *America, Russia, and the Cold War 1945-1992*, 7th edn, McGraw-Hill, New York, 1993.
49   Leffler, Melvyn, *A Preponderance of Power: National Security, The Truman Administration, and the Cold War*, Stanford University Press, Stanford, 1992.
50   Lenczowski, George, *American Presidents and the Middle East*, Duke University Press, Durham, NC, 1990.
51   Litwak, Robert S., *Détente and the Nixon Doctrine*, Cambridge University Press, Cambridge, 1984.
52   McCauley, Martin, *The Origins of the Cold War 1941-1949*, 2nd edn., Longman, London, 1995.
53   McCormick, Thomas L., *America's Half-Century*, Johns Hopkins University Press, Baltimore, 1989.
54   Matlock, Jack F. Jr., *Autopsy on an Empire*, Random House, New York, 1995 [memoirs of last US ambassador to Moscow].
55   MccGwire, Michael, *Perestroika and Soviet National Security*, The Brookings Institution, Washington, DC, 1991.
56   Menon, Rajan, *Soviet Power and the Third World*, Yale University Press, New Haven, 1986.
57   Nogee, J. l., and R. H. Donaldson, *Soviet Foreign Policy Since World War II*, 4th edn., Pergamon, New York, 1992.
58   Oberdorfer, Don, *The Turn: From Cold War to the New Era: The United States and the Soviet Union, 1983-1990*, Cape, London, 1992.
59   Paterson, Thomas, ed., *Kennedy's Quest for Victory*, Oxford University Press, New York, 1989.
60   Porter, Bruce D., *The USSR in Third World Conflicts*, Cambridge University Press, Cambridge, 1984.

61 Shambaugh, David, *Beautiful Imperialist,* Princeton University Press, Princeton, NJ, 1991 [on Chinese foreign policy].

62 Sick, Gary, *All Fall Down,* Tauris, London, 1985 [on America and Iran].

63 Shultz, George P., *Turmoil and Tragedy: My Years as Secretary of State,* Charles Scribner's, New York, 1993.

64 Stueck, William, *The Korean War: An International History,* Princeton University Press, Princeton, NJ, 1995.

65 Smith, Gaddis, *Morality, Reason and Power,* Hill and Wang, New York, 1986 [on Carter's foreign policy].

66 Taubman, William, *Stalin's American Policy,* Norton, New York, 1982.

67 Ulam, Adam, *Expansion and Coexistence, Soviet Foreign Policy 1917–1973,* 2nd edn, Holt, Rinehart and Winston, New York, 1974.

68 Vance, Cyrus, *Hard Choices,* Simon and Schuster, New York, 1983.

69 Young, John W., *Cold War Europe 1945–89: A Political History,* Edward Arnold, London, 1991.

70 Young, John W., *The Longman Companion to the Cold War and Détente,* Longman, London, 1993.

71 Zelikow, Philip, and Condoleeza Rice, *Germany Unified and Europe Transformed: A Study in Statecraft,* Harvard University Press, Cambridge, MA, 1995.

72 Zimmerman, William, *Soviet Perspectives on International Relations, 1956–1967,* Princeton University Press, Princeton, NJ, 1969.

73 Zubok, Vladislav, 'Khrushchev and the Berlin Crisis (1958–1962)', Working Paper no. 6, Cold War International History Project, Woodrow Wilson Center, Washington, DC, May 1993.

Territory annexed by USSR
1939-40 and reincorporated
in USSR in 1945

Former German and
Czechoslovak territory annexed
by USSR in 1945

States in which Communist
regimes came to power
between 1945 and 1948

The 'Iron Curtain' in 1955

| 0 | 500 mls |
| 0 | 300 km |

FINLAND

Vyborg

Jallion   • Leningrad

SWEDEN   ESTONIA

Pskov

Riga •   LATVIA

LITHUANIA

Konigsberg   Kaunas •   • Vilnius

Stettin   • Minsk

GDR
Since 1949   annexed by
Poland from
Germany

Bremen   Bialystok

SILESIA

Bonn   Berlin   Poznan   • Pinsk   SOVIET
UNION

Erfurt •   Dresden   Warsaw

GFR   POLAND

Nuremburg   Breslau

Prague   Cracow   Przemysl

CZECHOSLOVAKIA   GALICIA   Lvov

FRANCE   Munich •   Chernovtsy

Vienna   Uzhgorod

BESSARABIA

SWITZ.   AUSTRIA   Kishinyov

Jassy

Budapest
HUNGARY

Trieste   ROMANIA

Belgrade •   Bucharest

ITALY   YUGOSLAVIA   BULGARIA

Sofia

Tirane   ALBANIA

GREECE   TURKEY

GFR: German Federal Rupublic (West Germany)
GDR: German Democratic Rupublic (East Germany)

Map 1: The Soviet Union in Eastern Europe

Map 2: Eastern Europe since Communism

INDEX